THE
LIFE AND TEACHING
OF JESUS CHRIST

LONDON
Cambridge University Press
FETTER LANE

NEW YORK · TORONTO
BOMBAY · CALCUTTA · MADRAS
Macmillan

TOKYO
Maruzen Company Ltd

THE
LIFE AND TEACHING
OF JESUS CHRIST

by

CHARLES E. RAVEN, D.D.

Regius Professor of Divinity in the University of Cambridge

and

ELEANOR RAVEN

author of English History Studies
1485–1714

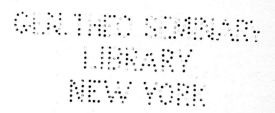

CAMBRIDGE

AT THE UNIVERSITY PRESS

1933

PRINTED IN GREAT BRITAIN

CONTENTS

II

PREFACE

This volume owes its appearance to a memorandum by Dr Nairne suggesting that the old type of commentary with its mass of detailed foot-notes was no longer wholly satisfactory. Its purpose is to give in condensed and simple form the necessary information as to the religious and social situation in Palestine, as to the evidence for the history of Jesus, and as to His life and teaching; and then to introduce the reader to the chief sources of our knowledge of Him. St Mark's Gospel and the primitive source 'Q' are set out in paragraphs with full references to the introductory material and brief notes on a few points of difficulty. These are supplemented by the chief portions of St Luke and St Matthew which add new evidence, and by a few passages from the earlier chapters of St John. We hope in this way to combine the advantages of the usual "Life of Christ" with those of a source-book; and to encourage readers to study the original documents for themselves.

Our thanks are due to Mr R. B. Henderson, and to the Syndics and officials of the Cambridge University Press.

C. E. R.
E. R.

July 1933

CHAPTER I

JUDAISM IN THE TIME OF OUR LORD

The Introductory Chapter is divided into three sections dealing with (A) the outline of Jewish history; (B) the development of Jewish religious beliefs; and (C) Judaism at the time of our Lord. Section A deals only with the historical events which are definitely connected with religion, and makes no attempt to give facts which are to be found in Old Testament histories. In Section B the growth of religion has been traced in such a way as to illustrate the influence of historical circumstances upon intellectual and religious life. It has not always been possible to keep separate the subject-matter of the two sections, but as far as possible repetition has been avoided. In Section C a short survey of Judaea at the time of Christ sums up the combined results of the two parts, and leads on to a consideration of Jewish religious beliefs of the same period; the more important of these beliefs has been explained, and their development, if not previously given in the earlier sections, has been outlined.

In addition to more general treatises the following will be found specially valuable:

- E. Bevan, *Jerusalem under the High Priests*.
- F. C. Burkitt, *Jewish and Christian Apocalypses*.
- R. H. Charles, *The Doctrine of a Future Life in Israel, in Judaism and in Christianity*.
- R. T. Herford, *Pharisaism*.

A. OUTLINE OF JEWISH HISTORY

The development of Jewish religious beliefs continued through the centuries of national history and was inseparably associated with external events and the circumstances of national life. The facts of Jewish history here given are outlined from the point of view of religious development; for an understanding of Judaism at the time of our Lord is important for the study of His Life and Teaching and cannot be gained without the help of some knowledge of its past history.

The Prophetic Teaching. Pre-exilic. In the years preceding the Exile (586 B.C.) the prophets were the great figures of Jewish history, and the teaching which it was their life work to impress upon the people was the most important of all religious influences. Through Amos, Hosea, Isaiah and Jeremiah a revelation of Jehovah was successively carried forward, and the identification of religion with goodness, which was characteristic of the prophetic message, was increasingly established. In the later days of Jeremiah the Captivity and Exile destroyed for many generations Jewish national life.

The Captivity and Exile. Old Testament history in the books of Kings and Chronicles gives clearly the record of the misdoings of rulers and people which led to the fulfilment by Nebuchadnezzar of the prophecies of Jeremiah. The Babylonian prince (Nebuchadnezzar's father was then upon the throne) defeated the Egyptians, the allies of Israel, at the battle of Carchemish in 605 B.C., and subsequently marched against Jerusalem. The city was taken and great numbers of the Jews sent captive into Babylon. In this time of Exile Jewish faith was kept alive by the prophet of the Exile, Ezekiel, who had himself gone into captivity with the first prisoners at the time of Jehoiachin's surrender (2 Kings xxiv). His work was continued, when a return to Jerusalem became possible, by the great prophet, who is called the Second Isaiah because his writings are included in chapters xl–lxvi of the biblical book of Isaiah and his own name is unknown. Babylon was conquered by Cyrus of Persia in 538 B.C., and Cyrus seems to have allowed the Jews to return to rebuild Jerusalem. Little or nothing is known historically of this return which had been hailed by the Second Isaiah with such hope and exultation, or of the Jews in the years immediately following it, but the books of Ezra and Nehemiah recount the later return under Artaxerxes, which is generally considered to have taken place about the year 430 B.C. This revival of religious life was of the greatest importance in the development of Judaism.

The growth of Legalism in post-exilic Judaism. It is to Ezra and Nehemiah and their predecessor Ezekiel that the emphasis upon Legalism or the supreme influence of the Law is chiefly due. Ezekiel had dwelt much upon the wickedness of the people and the need to build up a nation freed from iniquity; but in this new nation he had foreseen a priestly community in which the holiness of God should be preserved by a system of ritual and worship, having for its centre the new Temple, and so ordered that the people by its means might be kept holy and fit to serve a holy God. Ezekiel's outlook was confined to the idea of Israel as the chosen people; although he asserts the sovereignty of Jehovah over the nations, his vision in contrast to that of the Second Isaiah was a narrow and exclusive one. He aimed at combining the prophetic teaching with the setting up of an organisation which should express it in the national life, and safeguard it by means of external discipline and obedience to lawful authority. Idolatry, a very present danger in Ezekiel's time, was to be combated by giving the people ceremonies and ritual in a restored and purified Temple and by revising the Law and traditions. The imagery which expresses his ideas for reformation illustrates the passing from the prophetic to the Apocalyptic[1] age, for as the successor of the prophets he was also the forerunner of Daniel and Enoch; and the vision took the place of the prophet's message, as a manifestation of the will of God. Under Ezra and Nehemiah, Ezekiel's ideal was put into practice. During the Exile there had been a codifying of the Law, which under Ezra, the priest and scribe, took shape as the Priestly Code, including Leviticus, the later chapters of Exodus and the legal parts of Numbers. Certain chapters in Leviticus (xvii–xxvi) were known as "the Law of Holiness", and the whole code was insistent upon the holiness of Jehovah and His demand for the holiness of His people. As the fulfilment of the obligations of the Law became increasingly the service required by Jehovah from them, there arose the danger of a merely formal religion, an

---

[1] This word is derived from the visions or revelations (Apocalypses) which took the place of prophecy. For its significance see below, pp. 15, 16, etc.

obedience to the letter without regard to the spirit,
which characterised the priestly and Pharisaic religion
of the time of Christ.

For the remainder of the Persian period of Jewish
history, that is until the conquests of Alexander, there
is little available historical material. The Jews were
without political power or national independence, and
devoted themselves to the practice of their religion with
a zeal which strengthened Judaism to resist the dis-
rupting forces of Greek culture, with which from that
time onwards it came into contact.

The Jews and the Greek World. By the defeat of the
Persians by Alexander at Arbela 331 B.C., Palestine
became a part of the Macedonian Empire, and subsequently the bone of contention between Syria, which
after Alexander's death was ruled by the Seleucid
monarchs, and Egypt under the Ptolemies. It lay
between these two countries and was desired by both.
From 320 to 198 B.C. it was ruled by the Ptolemies; in
the years following it became a possession of Syria until
the Maccabean revolt. During all this time the Jews
were brought directly into touch with Hellenism. In
growing numbers they were attracted to Alexandria and
at the university there met at first hand Greek philosophy
and speculative thought, in an atmosphere wholly different from the nationalism and exclusiveness of Jewish
surroundings. As a consequence of this there developed
a series of writings known as the Wisdom Literature,
which shows clearly the traces of foreign influence and
includes such widely different books as Ecclesiastes and
Ecclesiasticus. During this period and probably in the

reign of Ptolemy Philadelphus (284–246 B.C.) was begun the Greek version of the Old Testament called the Septuagint, which had so great an influence in interpreting the religion of Israel to the Gentile world and in promoting the spread of Christianity. During it also the Dispersion or settlement of Jews in places outside Palestine was greatly extended; and this too was important for the preaching of the Christian missionaries. From submergence beneath the powerful Hellenising forces the Jews were rescued by the political events of their history. Under Antiochus Epiphanes, 175–164 B.C., and with the support of the high priest, a deliberate attempt was made to introduce Greek dress, customs and religion, and when this provoked resistance the king set himself to extirpate the Jewish faith. His persecutions aroused the revolt of Mattathias, the father of the five great Maccabean leaders, who at length won freedom for Israel. It was most probably during those days of trial that the book of Daniel was written to strengthen Jewish loyalty and hold out to the afflicted people a hope of comfort in a future life. Daniel's vision is indeed only of a partial resurrection, in which the righteous alone will inherit the Messianic kingdom, but the Messianic Hope which is so prominent in the writings called Apocalyptic was a great means of keeping alive Jewish religion.

The Jews and the Roman World. At Magnesia in 190 B.C. the Romans had defeated Antiochus the Great of Syria, and Roman intervention in the East began. The Jews under their Maccabean leaders had already approached Rome for a protective alliance, and Jonathan, who had succeeded his brother, the warrior king Judas, arranged such a treaty with the Roman Senate. Simon, the third Maccabee, was confirmed in his office as high priest and governor of the Jewish commonwealth by the Syrian ruler in consequence of this alliance. A time of prosperity began for the long-tormented Jewish race, but under it the people soon became secularised and forgetful of their religious vocation. Judaism was extended by conquest under succeeding rulers, and it was to combat the growing irreligion which this absorption in political matters was fostering that the separated party, the Pharisees, withdrew themselves more and more from contact with the Gentiles, and in consequence began to assume an attitude of superiority towards their fellow-countrymen which was in time to make the name of Pharisee proverbial for spiritual pride.

Jewish independence was ended by Rome at the instigation of Antipater, the Idumean and father of Herod the Great, at a time when the great-grandsons of Simon Maccabaeus were rival claimants for the throne. One of them, John Hyrcanus, who had been expelled by his brother, was supported by Rome. Pompey captured Jerusalem in 63 B.C. and reinstated him; Antipater was made procurator; Palestine was divided into five districts and attached to the Roman province of Syria. In the time of Julius Caesar the Jews were well treated and allowed exceptional privileges, such as permission to pay the Temple tribute. After 44 B.C. the Idumean rulers, Phasael governor of Jerusalem and his brother Herod governor of Galilee (Antipater being then dead), were favoured, and confirmed as tetrarchs by Antonius (Mark

Antony) then ruling the East under the Triumvirate. Idumean supremacy was intolerable to the Jews, and risings, aided by Parthia, temporarily evicted Herod and led to the death of Phasael. Herod then enlisted the help of Octavian and was restored with the title of king by Roman authority, taking Jerusalem in 37 B.C. He thenceforth retained his throne securely by the will of Rome, dazzling the people by his magnificence and horrifying them by his cruelties. In spite of the lifelong hatred of his subjects, Herod did much for the country, establishing peace and order and expending his wealth upon the rebuilding of the Temple. So bitter, nevertheless, was Jewish detestation that the day of his death in 4 B.C. was commemorated by them as a feast of national rejoicing.

After his death the seeming prosperity of Judaea rapidly disappeared. Three of his sons the king had himself done to death, but six still survived, and of these three had been nominated in Herod's will to divide the country between them. To Archelaus was given Judaea and Samaria; Herod Antipas received Galilee and Peraea with the title of tetrarch; Philip the tetrarchy of Trachonitis with other adjacent districts. Few traces of family affection are to be found in the story of the Herods, and the discord which had always haunted the blood-stained domestic life of Herod the Great was still further increased by their jealousies. Among the risings of that unhappy time was that of Judas the Galilean, which, though Judas himself escaped, brought Roman vengeance hard upon Galilee.

Archelaus reigned from 4 B.C. to A.D. 6, in which year he was dethroned by Roman decree for his misdeeds.

Judaea was taken under the immediate rule of the Roman Emperor; a procurator was appointed with a garrison of troops; the political importance of the Jewish Sanhedrin or State Assembly was much diminished; and a system of taxation, based upon the population and the estimated resources of the country, was imposed, which provoked a universal hatred extending to all even remotely connected with its organisation.

When Octavian became the Emperor Augustus in 27 B.C. his greatest work had been to reorganise the provincial government of the Empire. As commander-in-chief or imperator, he took under his personal control the provinces requiring an army, leaving the older and more peaceful areas to the Senate. In the imperial provinces, as in Syria, he appointed *legati* or governors, the title given by St Luke (ii. 2) to Cyrenius,[1] and under them or in smaller districts *procuratores*. These were men of equestrian rank, trained in the civil service, and usually of large experience and tested character. Their direct dependence upon the Emperor checked the opportunities for extortion and cruelty which had disgraced the administration in the days of the Roman republic; for their careers depended upon his favour, and upon a quiet tenure of office; outbreaks of revolt or complaints of disloyalty might be fatal to them, as we see in the case of Pilate. He was the fifth procurator and was appointed in A.D. 26. His attempt to introduce the imperial standards and emblems into Jerusalem provoked an outbreak early

[1] There is much uncertainty as to the date and the exact position of Cyrenius (Quirinius). He was certainly *legatus* of Syria in A.D. 6, and may have held a temporary appointment there earlier.

in his career, and his tenure of office was neither popular nor peaceable. His attitude at the trial of Jesus illustrates the difficulty of his position and his desire at once to prevent a breach of the peace and to maintain his own dignity. The Jews with their intense nationalism and sensitiveness to anything savouring of idolatry were a difficult people to govern. Pilate's long tenure of office (A.D. 26–36) proves that he was not wholly unsuccessful.

Taxation followed absorption into the Empire, and though the system was less iniquitous than in the days of Verres its administration was always extortionate. The collection of taxes in each province was taken over by one or other of the public contractors (*publicani*) at Rome: they paid over a fixed sum for the privilege, and appointed local agents, hence also called "publicans" in the Authorised Version of the Gospels, to collect it, and to make such profit as was possible.

The Romans though making Judaea and Samaria into a province left the two Herods, Antipas and Philip, in their tetrarchies. Antipas divorced his first wife, the daughter of Aretas of Arabia (cf. 2 Cor. xi. 32), in order to marry Herodias, his half-niece, who had been wife of his half-brother, another Herod perhaps also called Philip but certainly not the tetrarch (cf. Mk. vi. 17). John the Baptist, who like most Jews was scandalised by this, protested, was imprisoned and finally put to death. Both Antipas and Philip were great builders, the former establishing Tiberias on the sea of Galilee, called after the Emperor Tiberius, the latter Caesarea Philippi (Mk. viii. 27) and Bethsaida Julias (Mk. vi. 45; viii. 22).

B. OUTLINE OF THE DEVELOPMENT OF JEWISH RELIGION

Religious teaching of the Prophets. The religious teaching given to the Jews by the prophets was the chief influence which developed pre-exilic Judaism, and had a lasting effect upon all later Jewish thought. Of all the nations of the ancient world the Jews were pre-eminently devoted to religion, and from early days their faith became monotheistic. Their religious history for generations was a lifelong struggle against the idolatrous beliefs of polytheism, by which they were surrounded in the Promised Land. It was mainly the work of the prophets to keep the people faithful to Jehovah. Their teaching revealed Him as a righteous God caring for His people, identified righteousness with goodness, and proclaimed the need for right conduct as a duty above that of sacrificial offerings and the performance of ceremonial worship. Because the Israelites put their trust in the multitude of their sacrifices while their transgression continued unchecked, their condemnation was again and again denounced. In yet another direction prophetic teaching set itself against popular belief. It was a cherished conviction of the Israelites that the bond of union between Jehovah and His people was indestructible, and that as Israel could not live without Jehovah, so Jehovah would never abandon Israel. This relation did not appear to them, as it did to the prophets, in the nature of a moral tie, but as a fact accomplished once and for all by the covenant which had created the union. Such a belief was vehemently contradicted by the prophets. Only by fulfilling Jehovah's commands could Israel remain in fellowship with Him; should they transgress, the bond is broken; and should they continue obdurate in transgression, their rejection is unhesitatingly foretold.

This endeavour to turn the people into the right way was not the whole of the message of the prophets. In their belief Israel was indeed a chosen nation, but this privilege was to be the means of accomplishing Jehovah's purpose to the world, and was not simply the sign of His exclusive favour to the Hebrews. That through Israel the divine will might be known among the nations, Israel had been called. This ideal of universalism, that God was the God of all mankind, reached its highest realisation in the words of the Second Isaiah. We can trace in him and in Jeremiah the final stage in the process by which the God of Abraham and Moses, the God of Israel, became the Lord of all the earth in whom all mankind should be blessed.

The ideas of God embodied in the prophetic writings are those which come nearest to the teaching of Christ. They differed widely from the so-called Legalism, or religion of the Law, which grew up among the Jews after the Exile, and which our Lord found so generally held by the religious leaders of His own time.

Legalism and the Religion of Torah. Ezra had set before the people the ideal of following individually the will of God revealed to them in the books of Moses, the proclamation of which had been the chief act of his religious reformation. The form of Judaism known as the religion of the Torah (the Hebrew word means Teaching and not

Law), which set itself to a fulfilment of God's commands given in the written law, was the true descendant of Ezra's religion. From it there grew up the system of interpretation of the Torah and its explanation in the Tradition of the Elders (Mk. vii. 3, etc.), and the schools of the Rabbis or Scribes. These Scribes and Wise men (*Sopherim*), acting in consultation and according to prescribed methods, collected decisions and comments upon the Torah which were intended to enlighten and teach the nation. Such additions were not written down, for there could be nothing added to the Law, but were kept in memory and handed on from generation to generation. The Pharisees of a later time looked upon them as a part of the Torah itself, in the sense that they were the unfolding of the divine thought behind the written word. The Torah therefore in theory was an inexhaustible source of guidance, and by study and attention fresh realisations of its meanings could be learned. A part only of it dealt with rules and regulations of conduct, much of it was concerned with Jehovah and His attributes, with sin and restoration and with the last things. The Pharisees by unduly devoting themselves to the former section gave rise to the idea that Torah meant only Law and was confined to a series of commands and prohibitions. The formalism which under the Pharisaic system became so associated with religion was a perversion of Torah, and in no sense its real meaning or the true attitude to which it gave rise.

By means of the teaching and worship of the Synagogues the Torah was made known to the people, for all Jews, however far removed from Jerusalem and the

Temple, were linked up to the Holy City and its schools by the local Synagogue, where regular meetings were held for the faithful and their converts or proselytes. Its worship was not priestly or sacrificial like that of the Temple; its services of prayer and praise, lessons and instruction, supplied the model for the Christian Church; its government was in the hands of a "ruler" and a council of elders; in the absence of a regular Rabbi or Scribe any qualified person might be asked to speak in it. Jesus, although not a Rabbi, was thus enabled to begin the work of His ministry by preaching in the Synagogues of Galilee.

Messianic and Apocalyptic teaching. In the new religious conceptions the sacred writings of Israel were of chief importance, but there developed also a literature which centred around the Messianic Hope, and did much to keep alive religious faith. This Messianic Hope included beliefs which were widely held at the time of our Lord about the Messianic kingdom and the Person of the Messiah; beliefs open to more than one interpretation and coloured by political circumstances. They were of vital importance to the Jews in the midst of the Greek and Syrian influences with which their life was surrounded in the centuries before Christ, and the Apocalyptic literature which grew up from them had influence in developing the thought of the early Christians (for details of the Messianic Hope, see pp. 26–8).

Apocalyptic teaching carried forward in post-exilic times the religious ideas first given by the prophets. Both were concerned with revealing the will of God, and both were ethical in character. But Apocalyptic writers could not come before the people in their own name; for the canon of prophetic books was now closed, and the Jews believed that Jehovah had given His last word to His people, and that the work of later writers was to give interpretations of the scripture or decide problems about legal practices. If men therefore were conscious of an inspired message, they had to use the name of some venerated teacher of the past, and in that guise present their revelation to the people. There were therefore apocalyptic writings ascribed to Daniel and Enoch, Baruch and Moses, and others, of which the two first-named are important for the study of the New Testament.

C. JUDAISM AT THE TIME OF CHRIST

As will be evident from this survey of its history, the religion of Israel had developed greatly during the centuries since the Exile. In the religion of the Old Testament there are three chief elements—the Law developing out of the idea of a covenant with the chosen people, the Temple and its sacrifices and festivals, and the teaching and schools of the prophets. After the return from Babylon all these were modified both by deliberate reform and by the influence of events. The Law, interpreted by the Scribes and taught in the Synagogues, had been expanded into a system of worship and conduct almost independent of sacrifices or of any local ties, and fit to become the foundation of later Judaism when the Holy City was destroyed and the Jews driven out of Palestine. The Temple, though restored to splendour by Herod and possessing great prestige, was no longer the centre of vital religion: its day was nearly over. The prophetic succession had given place to the Rabbinical Schools of the Scribes, and to the Apocalyptic writers: its insistence upon righteousness had powerfully influenced the interpretation of the Law, and its passionate protest against oppression, its assurance of coming judgment, and its insistence upon the faithfulness of God and the triumph of His saints had been taken up by the Apocalyptists. The appearance of John the Baptist, in whom the people recognised a last prophet, proves that the prophetic spirit was still alive and powerful.

Judaism, then, at the time of our Lord, was ready for rapid change: the various elements in it were already splitting apart: after centuries of slow growth a time of decision had come which would sift out the good from the bad, test the worth of previous developments, and "judge" the people. The preparation was complete: out of the long agony and tension of Israel was to be born the Christian Church. The story of Jesus shows how He gave new and unique expression to the hope of Israel and brought its aspirations to fulfilment: the tragedy of it is the failure of the Scribes and the Synagogues to recognise His claim upon them.

To understand the event and to study His life in its surroundings we must survey the state of parties in Palestine during His ministry, and note the chief characteristics of their religious beliefs.

Judaea at the time of Christ was full of discontent and disorder. The country politically was a part of the Roman Empire, and the Jews were no longer a united nation, nor able except at moments of extreme excitement to act together. Distinct from the general mass of the Jewish people there were parties of Pharisees, Sadducees, Essenes, Zealots and Herodians, as well as Gentile peoples and proselytes (converts to Judaism) of Syria or Greece or Rome, and the half-Jewish half-Gentile Samaritans. Over such a population Rome had established the foreign dynasty of the Idumean Herods, and for this reason and because Herod represented Roman government and power, he and his followers, the Herodians, were detested by the Jews. The Herodians are only rarely mentioned in the Gospels, and the term is usually applied to the officers of Herod Antipas (cf. Mk. iii. 6; xii. 13). Probably they were in no sense a religious party and possibly may not have been Jews. But even national opposition to Roman influence was disunited; it was, indeed, torn by political factions and religious disagreement, for the parties of Pharisees and Sadducees were constantly in opposition to one another.

Jewish Sects and Parties. The Sadducees were a group of aristocratic families associated with the rule of the later Maccabean princes, who desired the political independence of Israel, but with that end in view were prepared to wait and assimilate Gentile culture. Though like the Pharisees devotees of the Law, they were bitterly opposed to them in rejecting the authority of all its traditional interpretations. Holding only to the five books of Moses, they refused all that could not be found in them, including belief in any resurrection (Mk. xii. 18). The name Sadducees, said to have been taken from that of the priestly Zadok, indicated that theirs was the priestly party, which controlled the Temple and its services. As all devout Jews paid the half-shekel for its support and made pilgrimage to it at the great festivals, this control, together with their wealth and social status, gave them a dominant influence in Jerusalem. Chief among them in the time of our Lord was Annas (Lk. iii. 2), high priest A.D. 6–15, father of four high priests and father-in-law of Caiaphas (Jn. xviii. 13) who held the office from A.D. 18 to 36. As we see from the Gospels (Mk. xi. 18), they were hostile to Jesus not only because of His teaching, but from His cleansing of the Temple-market. This was held in order to supply worshippers with the necessary victims for sacrifice and the sacred coinage for offerings; but brought much profit to the authorities as a monopoly.

The Pharisees were not strictly speaking a political party; for they did not, like the Sadducees, profess a definite national policy but concentrated upon the advocacy of religious principles. The Pharisaic hope was that of a Messianic time in which God alone should be King in Israel, and the chief power in the Sanhedrin, the governing agency of the country, should be in their hands. Numerically they were not strong, but their religious influence through the schools of the Rabbis or Scribes was very great, and they were the only religious party who tried by means of Synagogue worship to teach the people the Torah. Pharisee meant Separated, and the separation which was the true meaning of Pharisaism was that which came through complete devotion to the Torah as the way of service to Jehovah. Accepting the Torah as the divine revelation, the Pharisees sought to find in it not so much the meaning which the writer had in mind or had intended to make clear, as the meaning which the words had for them in their own time and circumstances. In laying stress upon its precepts the Pharisees made much of the importance of conduct, believing that by his actions a man could carry out the will of God which was made known to him, and to that extent devote himself to the forwarding of the divine purpose in the world. It was from the stress laid by Pharisaic teaching upon the exact performance of particular duties, that there arose the hypocrisy which was the ground of our Lord's chiefest condemnation.

Of more recent growth than Pharisees or Sadducees were the Essenes and Zealots. Both sects were the outcome of the social and political conditions of Palestine, and represented a reaction, though in exactly opposite ways, against the oppression and misgovernment of the land. The Essenes, of whom we know very little, withdrew into isolation and solitude in despair of being able to practise religion in the social life of the town. They founded communities devoted to a strict and ascetic rule of life, believing that only by withdrawal from the world could they serve God and keep their religion pure. Abandoning thus the burdens and responsibilities of life they had very little influence upon Judaism. There is no mention and no certain allusion to them in the Gospels, and the theory that Jesus was influenced by their teaching is mere guesswork.

The Zealots faced the problems of the time in a wholly different manner. The name came from a Hebrew word meaning one who was zealous, and is most nearly rendered into English by the term fanatic. In origin they were a religious party, but their beliefs centred in an intensely strong nationalism, and though like the other parties they accepted the Torah, they existed to fight and if need be to die for it, and were not concerned with its teaching or explanation. In this way they differed from the Pharisees who were opposed to violence, and the two bodies never coalesced. As the Zealot influence was strongest in Galilee, where there were few Pharisees and probably no Sadducees, theirs was the party with whom our Lord had opportunities of frequent contact, and one of the Twelve was distinguished by name as Simon the Zealot or Canaanean (Mk. iii. 18). A reference to Zealot activity may perhaps underlie the Lord's words in St Matthew that "the kingdom of heaven suffereth violence, and the violent take it by force".

Members of these parties, as we have seen, by no means made up the whole Jewish population. The majority of the people were not indeed attached to any one of them and differed widely in their devotion to religion. Belief in the Torah was common to most Jews, but while there were doubtless some among the people reaching almost to the Pharisaic standard of piety, there were many others outside even the worship of the Synagogue, "the sheep without a shepherd" or "the lost sheep of the house of Israel" of our Lord's words. Popular sympathies were far more with the Pharisees and the Zealots than with the Sadducees or the Essenes. Though the Pharisees might look down upon the people, they undoubtedly exercised great influence over them, while the fiery patriotism of the Zealots commended itself to all who suffered under foreign rule, and could rely upon support in times of insurrection or national upheaval.

Under Roman rule the official representative of these varied sects was the Sanhedrin, the Senate or Great Council of Seventy at Jerusalem. Originally a municipal and priestly body, this had included Rabbis of the Pharisees since the time of Herod the Great, and was given judicial as well as consultative powers, but not the right to execute a sentence of death without reference to the Roman procurator. Its president was the high priest, and the Sadducees still kept a dominant position in it. The Gospels clearly state that the whole Sanhedrin was concerned in the trial of Jesus (cf. Mk. xv. 1), but the meeting was certainly hurried and the procedure possibly irregular. Though the Pharisees acquiesced in the verdict, the initiative and chief responsibility rests upon the Sadducees; for it was they who effected the arrest, convened the meeting, formulated the charge, and brought pressure upon Pilate to carry out the sentence.

It remains to consider some of the chief principles of Jewish belief held and taught in the Synagogues in the time of Christ. For it was in this school that He was trained, and from it that He was called to His ministry. If we know what His Jewish kinsmen thought about God, about sin and righteousness, about God's kingdom and the Messiah, about the future judgment and immortality, and about the power of Satan and the demons and angels, we shall see how far these ideas were adopted and how far changed by Jesus.

(1) *The Idea of God.* The clearest proof of the character

of a religion is the picture which it gives of God; for upon this depends the faith and practice which men think suitable for His service. The Jews with their genius for religion centred their best thought upon the knowledge of God; and in the Old Testament we can see how each change in their history affected their thought about Him and how fuller knowledge altered their beliefs and their way of life. From the God of the sacred tree or pillar to the God of the brazen serpent or the golden calf, from the God of a family to the God of a nation, they had advanced under the teaching of the great prophets to the idea of the God of heaven and earth, the one true God, whose kingdom would one day include all mankind. After the Exile their experience of idolatry and of the many gods of Greeks and Romans strengthened them in their belief that there was only one God and deepened their sense of His majesty and of the distance between Him and His creatures. Instead of picturing Him as a man who could walk with Adam in the garden or speak face to face with Moses, they now regarded it as wrong even to mention His name, and ascribed to His angels or messengers all His dealings with the world. Though the psalms are full of the sense of His care and of confident trust and communion, yet any claim by a human being to act for Him seemed to them blasphemy, as we see when Jesus told the paralytic that his sins were forgiven (Mk. ii. 7). Thus, even if in some parts of the Torah there is the faith that God is the Father, belief in an Incarnation or in any revelation of God in man was difficult, indeed almost impossible. It is a striking proof of the impression made by Jesus that His Jewish followers came to confess Him as Lord and God. No other people would have been less likely to do so.

Though there can easily be collected from Judaism phrases in which the teaching of Jesus is indicated, there is nothing that approaches His consistent vision of "our Father" or His message that God seeks and saves the lost.

(2) *Sin and Righteousness.* (*a*) A sense of the importance of right conduct had been characteristic of the religion of Israel from early times; and the prophets had perpetually reminded them that God was holy and just, and that man must put away all iniquity and transgression. Between God and His people was the covenant; His will was revealed in the Law; observance of His commandments was the duty of His people.

Here too there had been development. At first Israel believed that those born within the covenant were chosen and would be rewarded, and that the children of the covenant would prosper even if sometimes they were punished. The great problem of the Old Testament was concerned with the sufferings of the righteous: how was it that men of upright life and true religion were forsaken and afflicted? The Exile made this question very urgent; for hard facts upset the simple belief that only the bad were punished with misery on earth. Gradually it was taught first that rewards depended not upon privilege of birth or the piety of parents, but upon the individual's own conduct, and later that rewards even if not given on earth would be bestowed hereafter. Belief in a future life was strengthened by the conviction that since God was just and good men often died unrewarded a recompense must be made to them after death.

Yet even in our Lord's time the old idea that suffering was the sign of God's punishment for evil still survived, as we see in the case of the Galileans slain by Pilate (Lk. xiii. 1, 2) and in the question "Did this man sin, or his parents, that he was born blind?" (Jn. ix. 2).

(*b*) The influence of the Law, though it gave to the Jews a deep sense of sin and a high moral standard, yet tended to make them think in terms of special acts of sin or of virtue, rather than in terms of separation from or union with God. The great prophets had insisted that righteousness was a matter of the heart or whole disposition, and that to walk humbly with God was more than any sacrifice or festival. But the influence of the Torah stressed the vital importance both of moral and of ceremonial conduct, and this easily led to pride and complacency. Those who kept the letter of the Law might thus easily deny its spirit. The Pharisees quarrelled with Jesus because His disciples failed to observe all their rules of conduct: Jesus condemned the Pharisees for their exaggerated attention to details combined with blindness towards essentials.

But the supreme difference between Him and them is that for Him sin and righteousness always depend upon a personal relationship with God; sin is forgetfulness or rebellion, righteousness is obedience and communion. Sins are important as symptoms of a sinful state, but it is not enough to repent of particular sins unless the whole self is brought back into love and worship of God. Righteousness does not consist in keeping the Law or doing good acts, but in living as a child of the Father, in knowing and fulfilling the Father's will, in being perfect as the Father is perfect. Thus, while the Jewish teaching is largely negative "Thou shalt not", His is positive "Blessed are ye poor"; and while its motive is reward, His is love, the love of God which expresses itself inevitably in the love and service of men. It is easy to exaggerate the contrast: but their rejection of Him proves how real it is.

(3) *The Kingdom of God.* Israel had always cherished belief in God's reign and in themselves as His subjects. Visions of a world-wide kingdom with its centre in Jerusalem and a prince of the house of David as God's viceroy, a kingdom into which all the treasures of the Gentiles should be brought and whose sway all nations would acknowledge, had sustained the Jews in all the calamities of their history. But as their hope of earthly sovereignty was constantly unfulfilled, their faith took a different form. In the time of our Lord many of them had given up the idea of a kingdom of the familiar kind, and looked forward to the spreading of their religion in this world and the enjoyment of God's undisputed dominion hereafter. Others, however, and especially the Apocalyptists and Zealots who were influential in Galilee, continued to hope that either by divine intervention or by national effort God's kingdom would be visibly established. Probably few of them expected a literal fulfilment of the portents which the Apocalypses predicted when God should put an end to the present age; for Eastern language always employs vivid and violent images to describe dramatic events. But we can trace in the Gospels many signs of the hope that a Messiah (the Anointed or

the Christ) would soon appear and "restore again the kingdom to Israel" (Acts i. 6).

Of the Messiah very various expectations were held. To some he was to be a son of David (Mk. xii. 35), a second Solomon in all his glory: to others he was a super-human being, God's representative and viceroy. Such hopes, natural enough in an intensely religious people groaning under pagan rule, were closely connected with the belief in God's justice, with His judgment of man-kind, and with the fulfilment of His covenant with Israel. They represent the stalwart faith which refuses to believe in the failure of what it conceives to be God's purpose and can face calamity in the assurance that He will not forsake those who trust in Him.

As we shall see later, Jesus began His message with the assurance that God's kingdom was at hand and accepted for Himself the status of Messiah. How differently He interpreted both kingdom and Messiahship is clearly seen by the misunderstandings of His disciples and His condemnation by the authorities.

(4) *Immortality*. Alongside of the hope of a Messianic kingdom as the fulfilment of God's covenant with His nation, there was developed in the three centuries before Christ a definite belief in immortality for the individual. Such belief is wholly lacking in most of the Old Testa-ment, and was therefore denied by the conservative Sadducees. But, partly under Persian and later Greek influences, and partly because of the problem of the troubles of the righteous on earth, hints of a resurrection can be found in the latest prophets and psalms; and in the Rabbinic and Apocalyptic teaching these became explicit.

The idea of immortality was combined with those of a Messianic epoch, a future judgment, and of heaven and hell (Gehenna, the place of punishment or destruction, in contrast with Sheol or Hades, the place of departed spirits). It is perhaps possible to trace a development in the various Apocalyptic writings on these subjects, but in the time of our Lord there was no general agreement as to details. Some held only a resurrection of the righteous; some of the spirit only, others of spirit and body; some a resurrection into the Messianic kingdom for the righteous and before the final judgment for all men; some placed the judgment before the establishment of the kingdom, others after it. Probably, then as now, there was very great difference both in the beliefs themselves and in the way in which they were expected to be fulfilled.

Jesus Himself seems to have accepted the main lines of Jewish thought and used the familiar pictures of a final judgment (e.g. Mt. xxv. 31–46), of a Messianic banquet and kingdom (Lk. xiv. 15–24, Mt. xxii. 1–14), of Abraham's bosom and Gehenna (Lk. xvi. 23) and perhaps of a catastrophic end of the present age (Mk. xiii. 24–7). But His teaching never emphasises the details of the "last things", and much of it is hardly consistent with the belief that He understood them literally. He uses such ideas to express His sense of the vital importance of man's earthly life in determining his relation to God and to warn His hearers against the rejection of God's love by persistence in selfishness and sin.

(5) *Jewish belief in Supernatural Beings.* Demon worship is a part of primitive belief and common to all forms of religion. It inevitably arises with the early

development of religious apprehension. There are traces of it in the Old Testament, e.g. Azazel (Lev. xvi); in Apocalyptic literature Azazel appears (Enoch viii, ix) in the rôle of Satan leading the evil spirits, and in the succeeding literature while there is no mention of Azazel there is recurring reference to Satan. In the Old Testament supernatural beings are represented as seeing Jehovah, and as angels to carry out His commands. "The angel of the Lord" is a supernatural figure spoken of almost as a distinct deity, and a scheme of the angelic world was very exactly worked out by the Jews two centuries before Christ. In the Gospels angels are similarly conceived of as God's messengers, as immortal and as ministering to men and closely concerned with humanity.

Evil spirits are not mentioned in pre-exilic writings, and Jewish contact with Persia was probably a strong developing influence. Satan the Adversary appears by name soon after the return from Babylon, and is visualised as a kind of embodiment of all Israel's difficulties and frustrations, and the symbol of all opposition to the welfare of the Chosen People. With the development of thought around the Satanic idea came the introduction of the fallen angels. In the New Testament the place of Satan is similar to that held by him in pre-Christian thought. Jesus here as elsewhere uses the language familiar to His contemporaries, and clearly personifies the evils which afflict mankind as the Devil, their enemy. The relation of the Devil to God, and the arguments as to his origin and destiny, are nowhere discussed: his overthrow is constantly proclaimed.

The belief in demons, or spirits intermediate between God and mankind, was characteristic not only of the Jews but of the Graeco-Roman world. Luck, accidents, dreams and disease were supposed to be due to them; and any form of insanity or nervous weakness and many physical disorders were regarded as "possession". A vast variety of propitiatory rites, of incantations and exorcisms, of charms and talismans, accompanied this belief. Jesus accepted the idea of possession in some of His miracles: but His complete assurance of God's supremacy and His entire lack of any fear or any desire to avoid or propitiate are in strong contrast to the attitude of His time.

CHAPTER II

THE EVIDENCE FOR THE LIFE AND TEACHING OF CHRIST

This chapter gives a brief account of the documents from which our knowledge of the work of Jesus in the days of His flesh is derived. It explains the character of the text—St Mark's Gospel, Q, L and M—printed in this book, and describes what is known of their authorship. On this subject there is a very large literature. To supplement what is here stated reference should be made to the following:

F. C. Burkitt, *Earliest Sources for the Life of Jesus.*

K. Lake, *The Text of the New Testament.*

C. E. Raven, *Jesus and the Gospel of Love,* pp. 128–60.

B. H. Streeter, *The Four Gospels.*

V. Taylor, *The Formation of the Gospel Tradition.*

EVIDENCE FOR CHRIST'S LIFE AND TEACHING

Considering the contempt with which Roman society regarded the Jews and the obscurity of Judaea in their Empire, it is not surprising that there is little evidence for the life of Christ in non-Christian literature. Suetonius, who wrote the Lives of the Caesars, probably alludes to Him when he tells that Claudius expelled the Jews from Rome because of their "continual quarrelling at the instigation of Chrestus".[1] Tacitus, the historian, describing the persecution of Christians by Nero after the great fire in Rome, states that "Christ from whom they took their name had been put to death in the reign of Tiberius by the procurator Pontius Pilate".[2] Pliny the younger, in his famous letter to the Emperor Trajan, shows how widely Christianity had spread in Bithynia, the province of which he was then governor, but tells us nothing of Christ except that hymns were "sung to Him as God".[3] Otherwise there is nothing.

Nor do Jewish sources give anything of importance. The fall of Jerusalem left little evidence of the Jewish writings preceding it; and after it the revived Judaism was bitterly hostile and deliberately kept silence about Christianity. Josephus, the Jewish historian, is the only author who might have given us an account; and there is one paragraph and some few allusions in his works. But the genuineness of these, though now not so strongly denied as by scholars of the last generation, is by no means certain; and in any case they hardly add to our knowledge.

---

[1] *Claud.* 25. [2] *Annals*, xv, 44. [3] *Epistles*, x, 96.

These allusions, though they testify to the fact of Christ, do not tell us much. It is from the Christian scriptures preserved by the Church in the New Testament that our evidence is drawn. This collection, although its contents were not absolutely fixed until much later, was formed early in the second century A.D.; for, when the Apostles and their successors died, their writings were used to settle the teaching of the Church and to answer heretics and opponents. About A.D. 160 a harmony or single continuous narrative was composed by Tatian, a pupil of Justin Martyr, out of our four Gospels; and before A.D. 200 Irenaeus, bishop of Lyons, and a man of learning, argued that in the nature of things there must be four, our four, Gospels and no others. So by his time, and probably long before it, these were accepted as authoritative. Although in the other books and especially in the letters of St Paul we have a mass of evidence as to the existence and the transforming power of Jesus Christ, some information about His teaching, and a few important facts about His life, it is in the Gospels that we find our knowledge of His deeds and words in the days of His flesh.

Granted that the four were almost universally accepted by the middle of the second century, we have still to ask two questions: can we be sure that our text represents what its authors actually wrote? and can we discover when and by whom the several Gospels were composed?

A. THE TEXT OF THE GOSPELS

To answer the first question is the business of Textual Criticism, a science which has to be used for all ancient books. Before the invention of the printing-press every book had to be copied in manuscript. In the Roman Empire and later on in the Monasteries the work of copyist or scribe was a regular profession, and literature was preserved and circulated by them. We do not possess the original author's copy of any book of the ancient world, and very few manuscripts are older than the fourth century A.D. Hence for all of them we have to study the text in order to see how far our copies of it are identical and to discover where there is variation and which reading is most likely to be original. Scribes were liable to make mistakes, to alter words either accidentally or deliberately, or to insert into the text notes or glosses written by scholars in its margin.

The Gospels were first published in print by the great scholar Erasmus in A.D. 1516. But there had been a "received text", almost standardised, since about the year A.D. 400 as the result of a revision during the fourth century when Christianity became the religion of the Empire and there was a great demand for copies of the scriptures. This "received text" was not made scientifically, and in order to reach accuracy we must go behind it to the earlier sources of knowledge. These are three:

(1) The manuscripts older than the revision or uninfluenced by it. These are all written in capitals (hence called Uncial) on vellum, and the most important are

(i) ℵ (Aleph) or Codex Sinaiticus discovered in a monastery on Mount Sinai; (ii) B or Codex Vaticanus in Rome; (iii) A or Codex Alexandrinus in the British Museum; (iv) C or Codex Ephraemi in Paris, a palimpsest or book in which the original text has been covered with another writing; its version of the Gospels is not complete; (v) D or Codex Bezae in the University Library at Cambridge; this differs rather widely from the others in including what are called "Western" readings. Of these five the first two are the oldest and most important: where they agree their evidence is usually accepted as final.

(2) The Versions or translations from the original Greek into other languages. The most important are the Old Latin, made before Jerome produced the Vulgate Text in A.D. 384 and existing in two chief forms; the Old Syriac going back to the early third century and known to us in two manuscripts. These Versions often help us to decide which of two readings is the more likely to be original.

(3) Quotations from early Christian writers. In the books and sermons of the Fathers of the Church are many passages from the New Testament. Occasionally these are taken from a verse in which there is a disputed reading. This evidence is therefore valuable not only as showing the existence and authority of the books but in helping to determine the text.

From these three sources and by careful comparison it is generally possible to say with tolerable certainty what the original words of the author were. Long and thorough study has been devoted to this question during the past century, and except in a few and unimportant passages there is general agreement among competent scholars. The extent and results of their work can be seen by comparing the Authorised Version of our Bible with the Revised Version; and the latter is not likely to be seriously altered by fresh research.

A few illustrations from St Mark may help to explain the sort of problems with which Textual Criticism is concerned:

(*a*) In the two oldest manuscripts, ℵ and B, the Gospel ends at xvi. 8 with the words "for they were afraid". Four other manuscripts contain two alternative endings, that printed in our Bibles and another very much shorter. In the recently discovered Freer manuscript a different form of the longer ending is found. These endings are all very unlike in style to the rest of the Gospel. Almost certainly the original text ended at xvi. 8, and because this was evidently incomplete another paragraph was added. There is some evidence that the longer ending is the work of Aristion, a Christian of the second generation.

(*b*) In vii. 3, "except they wash *diligently*" (Authorised Version "*oft*"), a common Greek word meaning "frequently" is found in most manuscripts: in A, B, D and most of the Uncial manuscripts, a rare word meaning "with the fist" is found, and this is more likely to be correct, because it might naturally be changed by a scribe who found it difficult to understand. It probably means "ceremonially", that is, with the hand closed for water to be poured on it.

(*c*) In iii. 17, "Boanerges", the word is spelled

differently in many manuscripts. It cannot be derived from any word that means Sons of Thunder, and is probably an instance of corruption by a scribe or many scribes who did not recognise the original word and copied it wrongly. A similar instance of a word that cannot now be identified is "Dalmanutha" (viii. 10), where the parallel passage in St Matthew xv. 39 and several manuscripts of St Mark have "Magadan" or a word close to it.

B. THE AUTHORITY OF THE GOSPELS

Our second question deals with the problems of dating and authorship, of sources and authenticity, that is with Literary Criticism. We know from the preface to St Luke (i. 1, 2) that when he wrote many had already undertaken to set out a narrative based upon the testimony of eye-witnesses, and that he himself had traced out the evidence. We are justified therefore in assuming the existence of earlier documents and in enquiring whether such sources can be found in the Gospels. It has been a matter of long and intensive research among students of the New Testament to compare the various accounts in closest detail, to observe their points of contrast and similarity, and to disclose so far as is possible the story of their relationship and of the material preserved in them.

As a result of this research certain general conclusions have been securely established.

In the first place there is an evident difference between the three Gospels of St Matthew, St Mark and St Luke, and the fourth, that according to St John. This difference had indeed been noted in early times, and the chief points were set out by a critic at the beginning of the third century: but it is only in the past hundred years that acute controversy has arisen. The whole subject of the authorship, character and historical value of the Fourth Gospel is still hotly debated: but certain points are manifest.

The Gospel, though it adds to our knowledge of the length and locality of the Ministry, is concerned more with the inner meaning of the person and teaching of Jesus than with a history of His life. It seems to be the work of one who is looking back after a long life of meditation and of experience to the events which he describes. His own growing appreciation of their significance colours his memory. Certain scenes stand out vividly: certain utterances have become more clearly understood: certain convictions about the Master's purpose and His relation to God have taken shape and are plainly expressed. This makes his book immensely valuable as an interpretation: it reveals to us the full influence of Jesus as that influence came to be acknowledged. But its picture is that of an artist, not of a photographer; and we cannot easily decide how much of his account of the acts and words of Jesus has been modified by his own reflections. For the history the first three Gospels are our chief guide: in them we can trace the immediate impact of Jesus upon His contemporaries, the sequence of events, the development of different methods of teaching, the growth of understanding among the disciples and of hostility among the Jewish authorities in a way that is impossible in the Fourth Gospel.

The first three Gospels from their general similarity have been called the Synoptics. Study of a synopsis of them makes clear (*a*) that St Mark is the earliest and is used by both the others; (*b*) that St Matthew and St Luke had another written source besides St Mark—this is usually called Q (from *Quelle* = source); (*c*) that St Luke contains a considerable amount of material not found in any other Gospel; (*d*) that St Matthew though mainly dependent upon St Mark or Q has added some particulars of much importance. These four supply our text.

(*a*) Tradition names St Mark as the author of our Second Gospel, describes him as St Peter's interpreter, and records that he wrote down what he remembered of the Apostle's teaching. This is in agreement with what we know of St Mark, that his mother had a house at Jerusalem which was the meeting-place of the early Church (Acts xii. 12), that he accompanied St Paul on his first missionary journey (Acts xii. 25; xiii. 6), left him at Perga (Acts xiii. 13), then attached himself to his kinsman St Barnabas (Acts xv. 37–9; Col. iv. 10) and was afterwards reconciled to St Paul (Philem. 24; 2 Tim. iv. 11), and that he was dear to St Peter (1 Pet. v. 13). It is also corroborated by the Gospel which records little except the Galilean ministry and the last week in Jerusalem, at which St Peter was present. It is possible that the youth present in Gethsemane (Mk. xiv. 51–2) was the evangelist.

The Gospel is almost entirely contained in those of St Matthew and of St Luke, St Luke following St Mark's order closely and St Matthew rearranging its material according to subject-matter. Both the later evangelists modify St Mark's style, removing its harshness, improving its language, softening its allusions to the weaknesses of the disciples, and ignoring its hints of a sequence of events. A comparison of a passage such as the healing of the paralytic (Mk. ii. 1–12) with the similar narratives (Mt. ix. 1–8; Lk. v. 17–26) will illustrate their characteristic use of it. The Gospel originally ended with the words "for they were afraid" (xvi. 8) and must therefore have at one time survived in a single mutilated copy. It is probable that the discourse in ch. xiii came from a separate written source, and possible that St Mark had some knowledge of Q.

The date of the Gospel is certainly earlier than the fall of Jerusalem (A.D. 70) and if, as seems probable, St Luke gathered the material for his work at Caesarea during the two years of St Paul's imprisonment (Acts xxiv. 27), earlier than A.D. 58 and perhaps much earlier. The only objection to this is the tradition that the Gospel was composed at Rome either before or, as others declare, after St Peter's death; and this may well refer not to its composition but to its publication.

Alone among the Gospels it contains distinct indications of the sequence of events in Galilee, of the changes in the attitude of the authorities towards Jesus and the influence of these upon the method and locality of His Ministry. Its many graphic touches, descriptive of scenes, utterances and gestures, reflect the observation of an eye-witness. As compared with the other Synoptists, it is free from any tendency towards apologetic, is artless, spontaneous, uncritical, a record racy of the soil of Palestine and the more impressive from its homely language and simple structure. Yet the keynote of its portrait of Jesus is the word "authority", and those who represent St Mark as a lion have chosen his symbol happily.

(b) Our second document consists of the material common to St Matthew and St Luke. A comparison of the two Gospels makes it almost certain that they used the same written source (compare for example Mt. iii. 7–10 with Lk. iii. 7–9) and that this contained an account of John the Baptist, of the Temptation of Jesus, of much of His teaching, and of several incidents, but apparently not of the ministry in Judaea or of the Passion. Here as in the case of St Mark it is probable that St Luke, though he makes verbal changes, has kept the order of the source more closely than St Matthew. It may well be the case that some of the material peculiar to each of the two Gospels was also derived from Q. But, though the existence of such a document can hardly be doubted, its exact contents and the use made of it cannot be precisely fixed. With one or two exceptions our text contains only what occurs in both, and follows very closely that in St Luke's Gospel.[1] No doubt the evangelist modified its style as he did that of St Mark; and several scholars (notably Harnack in his book *The Sayings of Jesus*) have examined in detail all the differences between St Luke and St Matthew and tried to reconstruct the exact language of Q. Such reconstruction would demand a large amount of explanatory vindication, and would then be tentative and subjective. It seems best to print the

[1] It is very similar to that set out by Streeter (*The Four Gospels*, p. 291).

Q material in its Lucan form with as few changes as possible and these changes generally accepted.

Its authorship is unknown: its date must at least be earlier than that of the Gospels which used it and perhaps than St Mark: its importance is very great, containing as it does some of the most familiar and revealing of all the sayings of our Lord. Many scholars identify it with a writing mentioned by Papias, about A.D. 120, as called the Logia and written in Aramaic, the dialect of Hebrew spoken in Palestine in our Lord's days, by St Matthew. This is very uncertain; for Q contains incidents as well as sayings; Logia probably means Old Testament prophecies rather than words of Jesus; and our source as used by the evangelists was certainly in Greek.

Not only is Q probably the earliest evidence that we possess, it also reveals even more plainly than St Mark the mind and experience of Jesus and preserves much of His most characteristic teaching. It assumes but does not specially emphasise His miracles—as in the answer to the messengers of John the Baptist (Q, p. 169) or in the prelude to the Beelzebub section (p. 174).[1] It contains Apocalyptic warnings, but these are much less precise than in Mk. xiii. It lays stress upon the connection of Jesus with John the Baptist and upon the prophetic aspect of His ministry. In particular it preserves the great utterance (Q, p. 173) to which the final clause, only recorded in Mt. xi. 28–9, seems certainly to belong, and which more plainly than any other passage in the

[1] The verse narrating the healing of the centurion's servant is totally different in Mt. viii. 13 and Lk. vii. 10 and is probably not in Q.

Synoptists reflects the communion of Jesus with His Father and His claim to be "the Way, the Truth, and the Life". It is not concerned with chronology and has very few indications of time or place. In these respects it has strong points of resemblance to the Fourth Gospel.

(c) The portions of St Luke's Gospel peculiar to it, described for brevity by the symbol L, even if not derived from Q, have not only great intrinsic worth but are of high authority for the historian. In style they are among the most beautiful writings in the world; in character they display the tenderness, universality and simplicity of Christ; in contents they include a Birth narrative, many of the most important of the parables, and a full and largely independent account of the Crucifixion and Resurrection.

That they are the work of St Luke, the companion of St Paul, is not universally acknowledged: but a strong case can be stated for it. The Third Gospel and the Acts are certainly by the same hand: the "we" passages beginning with Acts xvi. 10 are identical in style with the rest of the books: if these passages are, as has been argued, an incorporated travel-diary, they must have been wholly rewritten by the author who used them: if so, he would obviously have altered the "we" unless he desired to give a false impression of his presence; and if he were this sort of person, he would have introduced his appearance with a flourish of trumpets instead of allowing the "we" to slip in casually and unheralded. The objections to the Lucan authorship depend only upon the beliefs (a) that the books are late in date—a belief based upon flimsy evidence and irreconcilable with the inconclusive ending of the Acts which can only be explained if the author did not yet know the result of St Paul's trial before Caesar; and (*b*) that the discrepancies between the Acts and the Epistles of St Paul are too great to allow us to suppose that a companion of St Paul wrote the Acts—a belief which greatly exaggerates the differences, takes no account either of the divergence in temperament between the two men or of the long periods of their separation, and is itself testimony to the worth and early date of the Acts, since a late compiler would certainly have known and followed some of the widely read Pauline letters.

L may therefore be confidently ascribed to St Luke; and he gives us many hints as to the sources of his knowledge. During St Paul's imprisonment he was in close touch with the Church at Jerusalem, where besides Q and probably St Mark's Gospel he would get evidence from eye-witnesses: he mentions his contact with Philip and his daughters at Caesarea, names Manaen, Herod's foster-brother, Joanna the wife of Chuza his steward, who may possibly have supplied the details about Herod peculiar to L, and describes his own dependence upon the testimony of reliable witnesses. The Birth narrative, which differs somewhat in style from the rest of his work, may have been derived from one of the women attendant upon our Lord or even, as has been frequently suggested, from His Mother. The Passion narrative with its account of the Last Supper and of the post-Resurrection appearances may owe something to St Paul, whose interest in these matters appears in the First Epistle to the Corinthians.

(*d*) Of the matter peculiar to our First Gospel,

referred to by the symbol M, the greater part consists of
short additions to material derived from St Mark or Q,
of notes of the fulfilment of prophecy, and of points of
interest to Christians engaged in controversy with their
opponents. This is of secondary importance as evidence
for the life and teaching of our Lord, and many scholars
regard it as of doubtful authenticity. The First Gospel,
more definitely than any other, is composed and arranged
with the intention of proving the case for Christianity
against unbelieving Jews: it presents Christ as Son of
David, a second Moses, the fulfilment of Law and
prophecy: it emphasises His denunciations of the
Pharisees and His warnings of disaster: it answers
current attacks upon His birth and resurrection: it in-
troduces elements which seem to reflect the opinions of
a later date: it groups the existing material in a formal
order, often in blocks of seven or three, so that condensed
versions of teaching, parables and miracles are put
together irrespective of chronological sequence.

Its author is almost certainly not St Matthew the
Apostle; for the Gospel shows hardly any signs of being
written by an eye-witness, and it is very difficult to
believe that one of the Twelve would have taken the bulk
of his material from St Mark and Q. Probably the title
"according to St Matthew" was given to it because the
Apostle had written either the collection of proof-texts
or Q: if so, a later editor combining St Matthew's work
with that of St Mark and with other sources might
naturally give this name to his book. Its date seems to
be earlier than the fall of Jerusalem in A.D. 70; for the
author is so much occupied with argument against the

Jews that he could hardly have failed to appeal to the disasters which befell them as proof of their error in rejecting Jesus if he had known of the sack of the Holy City and the destruction of the Temple.

Though less important for our purpose than the two other Synoptic Gospels, the book contains certain passages and records of teaching which seem to be entirely free from later additions and may well be derived from early evidence. The most significant of these appear in our text.

CHAPTER III

AN OUTLINE OF THE MINISTRY

This chapter attempts to make plain the sequence of events described in the Gospels; to trace the chain of cause and effect; and to show how Jesus met the changing attitude of the people. It is based upon St Mark's record and should be studied as a running commentary upon his text. The three chief divisions though not emphasised in the Gospel are sufficiently distinct: the activity and methods of Jesus differ in each of them: each corresponds to a characteristic type of teaching.

For further study reference may be made to:

J. F. Bethune-Baker, *The Christian Religion*, Part 1.

F. C. Burkitt, *Jesus Christ: an historical outline*.

A. C. Headlam, *Life and Teaching of Jesus Christ*.

H. D. A. Major, *Jesus by an Eyewitness*.

J. M. Thompson, *An English Synopsis*.

INTRODUCTORY

I. Its Scene

One of the most remarkable facts about the life and work of our Lord is our almost complete ignorance of His early years. Except for the stories of His birth given in the First and Third Gospels and the solitary incident of His visit to the Temple at the age of twelve, our records give no details and but few allusions. He was content to live with Joseph and Mary and a large family of brothers or half-brothers in the house of the carpenter of Nazareth. The little town lies in a hollow just north of the strange level plain of Esdraelon which runs westward from the low valley of the Jordan, between the escarpment of southern Galilee and the more broken hills of Samaria, and is only cut off from the sea by the long ridge of Carmel. This was the great trade-route from Mesopotamia to Egypt and from Damascus to the coast—the one easy highway between the massif of the Lebanon and the southern desert. If you climb the steep slope south of Nazareth and above the winding valley that leads from the plain to the town, the whole of Esdraelon lies at your feet and beyond it a tangle of foot-hills leading away to the distant summits of Ebal and Gerizim, and beyond to the hill-country of Judaea. If you climb the slope on the north of the town, the hills are closer and more rugged. The track to Cana and from Cana to the Lake of Tiberias winds round to the west under the peaks now called the Horns of Hattin to the small plain where the Crusaders met their disaster. From the plain it is not far to the brow of the hills surrounding the lake: from the brow its shore from Tiberias to the hot and fertile level of Gennesareth, to Magdala and Capernaum and so to its northern end, to Bethsaida and the slopes of Decapolis coming down to the water's edge, lies close below you. Over all, visible indeed from the Judaean boundary, splendid at Nazareth and overwhelmingly beautiful from the lake, stands the brooding ridge of Hermon, snow-clad when the rest of the landscape is ablaze with the golden glare of the sun upon the limestone. To-day the country is barren and stony, brilliant with dwarf irises and scarlet anemones for a few weeks in spring, but, save for the narrow strip along the western shore which widens into the little plain of Gennesareth, bare and unfertile, and quite incapable of supporting a large population. In our Lord's time it was probably more wooded and with more rainfall: the lake certainly supplied a trade in pickled fish, and the villages now few and poverty-stricken may well have been comparatively flourishing, though Josephus whose natural vanity led him to magnify his own status has almost certainly exaggerated their population.

II. Its Commencement

In this area, small, diversified and of mixed population, where Jewish nationalism and Greek culture lived uneasily together under Antipas the puppet of Rome, Jesus was content to stay until the coming of John the Baptist. Then when this latest born of the prophets drew multitudes to him, Jesus, perhaps accompanying friends from Galilee, went Himself to Jordan, was baptised and

received His call. What that call involved was made clear
in the weeks of solitude which He spent in the wilderness.
St Mark notes the fact: Q gives a dramatic and most
revealing account, in which the lines of His temptation
are intimately described. He will not use any of the
methods by which success is commonly achieved; He
will neither minister to the bodily and social needs of
men, nor appeal to force for their coercion, nor win their
admiration by a sign from heaven; the way of Moses and
the manna, of Caesar or the Zealots, of the Apocalyptists
and a Messiah descending on the clouds into the Temple,
are all rejected. We are not told how clearly He foresaw
and planned His own course: but His ministry shows
repeatedly that these three ways are closed. When people
seek Him for healing or food, He leaves them and retires
(Mk. i. 35–8; cf. Jn. vi. 15, 26): when they ask for thrones
or draw the sword, He rebukes them (Mk. x. 35–45;
Lk. xxii. 49–51): when a sign is demanded, He refuses
it (Mk. viii. 11–13; cf. Lk. xi. 29, 30). By word and act
He progressively discloses the alternative which He had
chosen.

THE MINISTRY OF JESUS

I. The First Phase: Public Ministry in Galilee

A. *The First Preaching*

Between the Temptation and the opening of the Ministry in the Synoptic record there is an interval; for
St Mark, describing the work in Capernaum, dates it
"after John's arrest" (Mk. i. 14). The Fourth Gospel

describes the call of certain disciples, the wedding at Cana and a visit to Capernaum, then a journey to Jerusalem for the Passover, the cleansing of the Temple and the visit of Nicodemus; then a period of baptising in Judaea while John was at Aenon near to Salim and "not yet cast into prison" (Jn. i. 35–iii. 36). The journey described in Jn. iv. 3 and the meeting with the woman of Samaria may be the same as that in Mk. i. 14; and the events of Jn. iv. 43–vi. 71 will then coincide in time with those of Mk. i. 14–ix. 50. The sequence of events in the Fourth Gospel is not easy to follow: but from the other accounts it seems probable that there had been a period of ministry in Judaea and perhaps visits to Galilee earlier than the point at which the Synoptists begin.

St Mark describes the proclamation of the good news of God's kingdom in Galilee, the call of Simon and Andrew and the sons of Zebedee, then in some detail a sabbath in Capernaum where the "authority" of Jesus in word and deed excites public enthusiasm, and then a preaching tour through Galilee, during which may be placed the visit to Nazareth recorded in L (Lk. iv. 16–30 which implies, *v.* 23, a previous visit to Capernaum).[1] This period may have been a long one and have included some of the teaching in the early part of Q or in St Matthew's Sermon on the Mount (Mt. v–vii). There was much interest and enthusiasm at the direct appeal of the new teacher. Jesus, though healing the sick, refuses to put this work first or to allow His cures to be advertised abroad. This is plainly seen in His injunction to the leper (Mk. i. 43–4).

[1] If Luke's order is correct, this visit may be that in Jn. ii. 12.

B. *The Growth of Hostility*

Galilee, always the centre of nationalist hopes, was violently excited: and the Rabbis or Scribes in charge of the local Synagogues were naturally interested in Jesus and His message. They had been looking for a leader, and now perhaps their hopes were to be fulfilled: yet Jesus was not one of their own order—neither Scribe nor Pharisee: they could not accept Him without long and careful testing. Suspicion of His orthodoxy was first aroused when He declared to the paralytic that his sins were forgiven. In so doing Jesus was in fact repudiating the current belief that disease was the visible proof of God's anger, and convincing the man that the Father was not vindictive but forgiving. Nevertheless, to the Rabbis to declare forgiveness was to usurp God's prerogatives. "This is blasphemy" was their murmured comment. Jesus vindicating the truth of His words by their effect might silence them, but they would watch Him jealously.

There follows a succession of incidents which increase their hostility. Jesus shared a publican's hospitality and declared that His mission is to "sinners", that is the "untouchables" outside the covenant. He defended His disciples for not observing a fast by two short parables which reveal the radical difference between His religion and that of orthodox Judaism.[1] He permitted and justified a technical breach of the Sabbath. Finally a testcase occurred in the Synagogue, a case evidently arranged by the authorities. St Mark describes their sidelong glances and expectation as Jesus is confronted with the

[1] For their significance cf. p. 86.

cripple. He goes at once to the heart of the matter: "Is the sabbath intended for human welfare and good deeds?" Grieved and indignant at their callous silence, He heals the man. The Pharisees at once open negotiations with Herod's officers, the local magistrates, instigating them against Him.

II. THE SECOND PHASE: THE TRAINING OF THE DISCIPLES; JOURNEYS OUTSIDE GALILEE

A. *The Appointment of the Twelve*

Local hostility in Galilee had thus become official, and a general public ministry there was consequently less practicable. Multitudes were now gathering from every part of the country, but in view of the attitude of the authorities a continuance of open proclamation of the kingdom would inevitably have produced a clash and strife. Jesus therefore deliberately prepared for a change of method. He withdrew into the hills, accompanied only by disciples specially chosen; and there appointed the Twelve to be missionaries with Him. His purpose was immediate and practical, the creation of a group on whose training He could concentrate, who could accompany Him if necessary away from the ferment in Galilee, and who would learn by constant intercourse, by observation as well as by instruction, to undertake service for the kingdom and so gain experience of its power. Though they formed in a sense the first nucleus of the Church, their office was one of function not necessarily of precedence; and it is notable that of most of them we know little and that neither James the first "bishop" of

Jerusalem nor Paul, Barnabas and Philip the Evangelist, the most effective missionaries of the early Church, were of their number.

After their appointment a more serious conflict with the authorities took place. The local Rabbis had apparently reported their difficulties to their leaders in Jerusalem, and a deputation (Mk. iii. 22) had been sent down to investigate. This had alarmed the relatives of Jesus who in their anxiety tried to get control of Him on the ground that He was out of His mind. The deputation took a similar but more hostile view. They could not deny His influence: they could represent it as diabolical. Hitherto the charges against Him had been His disregard of the ritual laws of fasting and the Sabbath. Now a more drastic attack was made: He was inspired not by God but by Beelzebub: His acts of mercy were the acts of a demon masquerading as an angel of light. Jesus faced with such a verdict uttered one of His most tremendous warnings: blasphemy need not mean complete loss of moral consciousness or a complete separation from God, and so can be forgiven: when it becomes a deliberate confusion of good with evil, a total blindness to moral worth, it involves a condition of estrangement in which forgiveness, the communion of the Father with His children, is cut off by their refusal to recognise Him. To the deputation His reply is uncompromising: to His mother and brethren He replies that the doing of God's will is the true bond of kinship.

B. *The Teaching of the Twelve*

(1) *The Method of Parables*. Public enthusiasm still continued; and Jesus developed a new type of teaching. In the presence of a crowd so large that He addressed them from a boat He told the parable of the Sower, and explained the method by a challenge to spiritual insight: "He that hath ears to hear, let him hear". His disciples, bewildered by what must have seemed to them an irrelevant story and a lost opportunity, questioned Him. He explained His intention of revealing to those who can see it the open secret or "mystery" of God's kingdom. Parables will not inflame the excitement of the people: to understand them requires a measure of sympathy and intelligence: they will thus sift His hearers, and develop the sensitiveness of His followers. The parable becomes His regular method of teaching from this time onward; and St Mark sets out four others illustrating different aspects of the kingdom. The message from John the Baptist and the incidents illustrating the cost and significance of discipleship (Q, pp. 169–71) probably reflect the excited questioning at this period of the ministry, the professions of enthusiasm, and the searching demands by which such enthusiasm was tested.

(2) *The Miracles*. In accordance with His policy of withdrawal He now crosses to the eastern shore of the lake at Gergesa, probably the modern Kersa.[1] The journey and return are associated with four miracles—the stilling of the storm, the healing of the demoniac, the healing of the woman with an issue of blood, and the

---

[1] Not Gerasa nor Gadara, which were big towns and far away.

raising of Jairus' daughter. These raise inevitably the question of the reality of miracles which has for so long been a source of perplexity. A full discussion would be out of place; but two points should be remembered: first that the contemporaries of Jesus had none of our scientific training, believed in miracles as firmly as in more normal events, expected them to happen and accepted them uncritically; and secondly that the character of Jesus was such that we should expect Him to possess unique influence and powers wholly beyond the range of less perfect personalities. These two points compel us to scrutinise the evidence carefully, making full allowance for the tendencies of the writers, and to refuse absolutely to assert that miracles are impossible because men of our type do not normally experience or perform them.

Thus in these four cases. It is obviously possible that in the first the disciples in fact exaggerated their danger, that the courage of their Master quieted the storm of their panic, and that the calming of wind and waves was due rather to a change in their appreciation than to a change of weather: or we may point to the suddenness and brevity of the tempests that break upon the lake as upon many lakes set among mountains: but we cannot exclude the possibility of the influence of Jesus; for we do not know if or to what extent inanimate nature is subject to such influence.

The second has long been a difficulty. Demoniac possession was then, as it is still in the East, regarded as a fact. Jesus seems to have accepted it as did all His contemporaries; and many students of psychic disease would to-day refuse to deny the possibility of such evil influences, though they would describe them rather in terms of obsession or of dissociation than of possession. That Jesus wrought a cure is in full accord with a mass of evidence as to His power: the difficulty does not lie there, but in the suggestion of the evangelists that the demons entered into the herd of swine. This is an inference which would certainly be drawn in those days if at the time of the cure the swine were excited and rushed over the cliff. That those who saw it jumped to the conclusion that their excitement was the work of the demons is natural enough: and if so, the story would be told so as to include this explanation. To argue that Jesus was morally responsible for the drowning of the herd is almost as absurd as to suggest that He did it because pig-keeping was a breach of the strict code of Judaism.

The fourth miracle is also of special interest. Here it seems clear that Jesus Himself declared that the child was not dead, but asleep. Though one Greek word for sleep, that from which cemetery is derived, is commonly used of death, Jesus uses the other ($\kappa\alpha\theta\epsilon\acute{\upsilon}\delta\epsilon\iota\nu$) which is normally literal in its meaning. He forbade the mourning, and roused the child from her swoon: but His followers, refusing to accept His statement, evidently supposed that she had been raised from the dead. Here is a case of a miracle which has been exaggerated in spite of the Master's explicit statement to the contrary.

The third resembles that of the healing of the demoniac or of the paralytic. Jesus, here as elsewhere, insists upon the importance of faith in the patient: modern experience, differing in that respect from the views of a generation ago, realises that where there is sincere expectation amazing results can be achieved: the cure need raise no problem. That Jesus should have been aware of it is only in accord with what we ought to expect. That He was sensitive, far beyond our limits, to the unspoken desires and motives of men is proved repeatedly by the evidence. He knows the hearts and reads the thoughts of men with an immediate intuition. He did so at the healing of the paralytic and with the cripple on the sabbath: we can see the same unerring insight in His answers to the questions in His last week at Jerusalem. Here as in His miracles He transcends our powers enormously: He possessed what we have never known, the influence of a manhood wholly at one with God: but if we can see in ourselves some faint analogy of His glorious "authority", we can realise that His miracles do not violate the "laws of nature" but reveal the operation of those laws as they apply under unique circumstances to an unique personality. We can see enough in our own experience to maintain that with Jesus such "miracles" are exactly what we should expect. They are no longer an obstacle but a confirmation to belief.

C. *The Mission of the Disciples*

Galilee was still full of excited speculation; Herod Antipas himself was interested, curious (Mk. vi. 14) and hostile (Lk. xiii. 31). The neighbourhood of the lake had become ill-suited to the purpose of Jesus. He therefore set out on a second tour with the disciples, and visited Nazareth—probably the visit described also in Lk. iv. 16–30. Meeting with unbelief and violence there, He travelled through other villages and afterwards sent out the Twelve "by two and two" on a similar mission, with the intention not only of covering a wider area, but of giving His disciples the opportunity to learn the worth of service and the power of their message. This mission is probably the same as that recorded in Q (pp. 171–3); for St Matthew combines the account there with that in St Mark (Mt. x. 1–15). It may well have lasted for some weeks, though we have no details either of its course or of the doings of Jesus during it. St Mark uses the interval to describe the death of John the Baptist.

Whatever its duration, the mission filled the disciples with enthusiasm and must have played an important part in their training. Jesus took them apart for quiet and probably at this time experienced the triumphant joy ("agalliasis") which is expressed in the great utterance in Q (p. 173) with its Johannine certainty of union with the Father, and its claim to unique relationship with Him and with mankind. The final stanza, though not recorded by St Luke, seems an authentic and necessary part of the utterance, expanding the claim and declaring the condition of its fulfilment for mankind. That such a self-revelation should have preceded the confession of St Peter and been given at a time of rest when a great venture had been faithfully performed is in keeping both with the "authority" of Jesus and with the course of the ministry: that the disciples did not yet grasp its significance is not surprising; for even when they had confessed His Messiahship they failed to understand the scope and the simplicity of His function.

Their retreat must have been to the east of the lake,

outside Herod's dominions and probably to Bethsaida Julias on the north-east shore (Lk. ix. 10, but Mk. vi. 45[1] apparently places Bethsaida on the western shore in Gennesareth). Here too crowds assembled, and at evening Jesus bade His disciples give them food. Five loaves and two fishes were produced, from a lad according to St John (vi. 9): but these may have been supplemented by the contents of the baskets which, as Juvenal[2] knew, devout Jews when travelling carried with them in order to observe the food-laws, and which are mentioned later in the narrative. Jesus took the loaves and fishes, blessed and brake and distributed them to the seated companies of people. The event is described in all four Gospels as a miracle: but St John shows it significance more plainly than the others. In his version it is clearly a ceremonial and eucharistic meal, similar to the Agapé of the early Church, and regarded by those partaking in it as an act of allegiance to Jesus; for after it the people wish to make Him King and He warns them that His work is spiritual and involves belief rather than material benefits (Jn. vi. 15, 26–8).

After the feeding of the five thousand the disciples were sent across the lake, and according to St Mark and St Matthew (St Luke does not include this nor anything in Mk. vi. 45–viii. 26) Jesus withdrew for prayer to the mountain and followed them later, walking on the sea. St Mark describes their alarm, His encouragement of them, and His reception into the boat: St Matthew adds

[1] The verse is difficult and has produced many unconvincing explanations. It is probable that "to Bethsaida" has been misplaced and should come in *v.* 32.

[2] "The Jews whose equipment is a bundle of hay and a basket."

the story of St Peter's attempt to join Him upon the water. St John's account is somewhat different and if it stood alone would not involve a miracle; for he describes how when they have almost crossed the lake they see Jesus "at" (or "on") the sea, desire to take Him into the boat, and find themselves "at" (or "on") the land.

D. *The Journey to the North*

The appearance of Jesus in Gennesareth was at once the occasion of fresh excitement: crowds followed Him, carrying their sick with them for healing. The Pharisees and the Rabbis from Jerusalem again attacked Him, on this occasion for transgressing the Tradition of the Elders. Clearly a crisis had arisen: popular expectation would have accepted Him as a national hero, and if He had compromised with the religious leaders they might have thrown in their lot with His cause. Not only did He accept their accusation, but He condemned the tradition explicitly on the ground that its provisions frustrated the fulfilment of God's law. He quoted the denunciation of Isaiah and illustrated His contention by the case of Corban: a man's primary obligation and God's evident law is the support of father and mother; to give offerings to the sacred treasury, when these ought to have been devoted to parents, is not to honour God but to ignore His will: the belief that a gift to religion is more important than natural duty and the fifth commandment is false and implies a mistaken outlook.[1] It is an essential element in

[1] Edersheim and many commentators suppose that Jesus is condemning Corban because a man pledged his money to God and then did not give it. Jewish scholars justly protest that this is a libel upon Rabbinism. It is not the meaning of the passage.

the religion of Jesus (as is shown later in His attitude to divorce, Mk. x. 5–12) that no man-made rules however august can be set against the principles of the natural order.

Having thus made clear His refusal to seek support from the Pharisees, Jesus proclaimed His opposition to them publicly: turning to address the crowd and claiming their earnest attention, He challenged the whole principle of the ceremonial law at its most rigid and elaborate point. Not what a man eats, but what he says—not what goes into the mouth, but what comes out of it—brings defilement. He had already shown that for Him the value of fasting or of the Sabbath was dependent upon their power to promote man's highest welfare, that rules of behaviour, however venerable, are secondary, that His whole concept of religion was based upon vital communion with God and not upon obedience to law. Now He defines and makes absolute His departure from the Judaism of the Rabbis. The food-laws were the obvious and most noticeable of the characteristics of Judaism: in rejecting them He set Himself outside the traditional tenets of His people. St Mark adds a note (vii. 19), "this utterance makes all meats clean", to indicate the revolutionary character of His announcement as He explained its import to His disciples.

Such a challenge must have involved immediate departure from Galilee, though it is likely that parts of the fourth section of Q (pp. 174–81) refer to the controversy on this occasion. After it He took the disciples on the longest of His journeys, travelling secretly to Tyre, where He healed the Syro-phoenician's daughter, through

Sidon and apparently across Lebanon into Decapolis, and so to the east side of the lake. If, as appears from the Fourth Gospel (Jn. vi. 4), the feeding of the five thousand was in the spring, much of the early summer may have been spent on this journey. The only incidents associated with it are the healing of the deaf man with the impediment in his speech, and the feeding of the four thousand—a story so similar to that of the five thousand that it may perhaps be another account of the same event.[1]

Crossing to Galilee the Pharisees again accosted Him. Only a direct sign from heaven can now vindicate Him. He refused it, returned to the boat, and left so hurriedly that food was forgotten. Events were moving to a climax, and although the disciples showed plainly how little they understood, the decisive step in their training must be taken.

E. *The Confession of St Peter*

He landed at Bethsaida, restored a blind man's sight, and set out to Caesarea Philippi, the new town which Herod Philip had built under the spurs of Hermon. Close up to the mountain whose beauty throws a spell over Galilee, among a mixed population where Jewish nationalism and Jewish orthodoxy would no longer distract His followers, Jesus brought their training to its test by a direct question. They had learnt slowly and with much misunderstanding to read the meaning of His parables, to see God in simple signs and sacraments. It

---

[1] St Mark and St Matthew clearly regard them as different, and they differ in detail—seven loaves, seven large baskets of fragments, instead of the five loaves and twelve small baskets of the earlier miracle.

was time for them to face the issue which had been raised by John the Baptist and no doubt debated in the turmoil of Galilee. "Whom say men that I am?" is the prelude to "Whom say ye?" Simon Peter, spokesman of the Twelve, answers "Thou art the Christ".

It belongs to our study of the teaching of Jesus to consider the precise meaning of the confession both as the Apostles understood or misunderstood it and as their Master exposed it to them. It marks a definite and decisive period in the ministry, and enabled Jesus to regard His work in Galilee as complete and to go up for His passion at Jerusalem. The fire was kindled upon the earth: He could engage on the last and most intense adventure.

But first having confessed Him they could see Him in His true stature. That is the significance of the Transfiguration. They had made the act of faith: by it their eyes were opened. The Christ was no longer only the Carpenter of Nazareth or the Son of Man: He was the fulfilment of the Law and the Prophets: Moses and Elijah would stand on either side of Him and the glory of the Shechinah, the light of God, would shine upon Him. So they saw Him on the Mount.

From it, as in Raphael's great picture, He descended with them to the distracted world of pain and hopeless woe, to the epileptic and his father; and met the wistful prayer "If you have the ability, help us" with His triumphant "Do you say ability? All things are within the ability of him who has faith", and with His act of healing. Confession, experience, power—the disciples who had known that threefold encouragement could surely face the future undismayed, even if the future was the Cross.

III. The Third Phase: The Crisis in Jerusalem

A. *The Preparation*

(1) *The Journey through Galilee.* In fact they were far from ready for what their Master saw before them. He had already warned them in the moment of their ecstasy that He would suffer and be set at naught. The rest of His dealing with them is concerned with two closely related though seemingly paradoxical lessons. They have confessed Him as the Christ: He can now put a new stress upon His own place in God's purpose, a new claim upon man's allegiance. But His Christhood is not that of a second Solomon but of Isaiah's suffering servant: His title to lordship is in a ministry of service unto death.

They passed secretly through Galilee and He taught them plainly of His betrayal and passion. He came to Capernaum, found them arguing which of them was the greatest, took a child in His arms and told them that greatness was in acts of love and mercy; found St John acting with exclusive intolerance, rebuked him and warned them of the awful importance of right decisions, and the peril of stumbling and causing others to stumble. Their choice is between life and destruction.[1] They are indeed the purifiers of the world; they will purify it as they learn to suffer and to love: otherwise the salt will lose its savour. Pride whether of precedence or of

---

[1] Gehenna is not necessarily the hell of unending torture but the refuse-heap on which offal is destroyed.

proprietary rights would destroy the essential quality of their work.

It seems probable, alike from the subsequent silence of St Mark and from the Fourth Gospel, that on the southern boundary of Galilee Jesus parted with the majority of His followers. St Luke describes certain incidents, the healing of lepers (xvii. 11–19) and the rejection (ix. 51–6) as occurring on the marches of Samaria; the Fourth Evangelist, who apparently narrates St Peter's Confession in vi. 68–9, then describes a visit to the Feast of Tabernacles, an autumn and winter in Jerusalem, an interval beyond the Jordan, a visit to Bethany, and a retreat to Ephraim, before the final Passover. If this sequence is correct, there must have been nearly six months between the departure from Galilee and the passion. Except Thomas (Jn. xi. 16) and perhaps the sons of Zebedee (Lk. ix. 54) no disciples are named during this time; and, judging by St Mark, St Peter was certainly not with Him.

(2) *The Journey to Jerusalem.* St Mark resumes his record with a verse of great importance. "Jesus went into the boundaries of Judaea and across the Jordan" may either be a summary of the Johannine account of a long sojourn in Judaea and in it a journey into Peraea, or it may describe His course as He goes from Samaria through Judaea to meet St Peter and the others at Jericho, a course which, as seen from St Peter's point of view on the ordinary pilgrim-route through Peraea,[1] would be also "on the far side of Jordan". Whichever is meant, on entering Judaea Jesus resumed the public

---

[1] To avoid Samaria the normal approach from Galilee to Jerusalem was along the east bank of Jordan to Jericho.

teaching of large crowds which, as the repeated "again" of the text shows, had been for some time abandoned.

Significant also is the question immediately raised by the Pharisees. The whole of Judaism had been horrified by the divorce of Herod Antipas and his remarriage to the wife of his brother. In Galilee and under Herod's own rule the subject was dangerous: directly Jesus enters Judaea He is confronted with it; and St Mark adds that the question was a test: whatever answer was given might be used to embroil Him with the religious authorities or with the Tetrarch.

Here, as in the Corban, Jesus appeals from the Mosaic law to the natural order and the story of the creation. Monogamy is involved in the complementary character of the two sexes. Man and woman are made for one another; and their union once accomplished is a fact which no legal enactments can alter. They have created a partnership, and, while both are alive, union of either of them with another is adulterous. That is the plain purpose of God and the plain meaning of the language of Genesis. Jesus Himself, as His attitude towards moral issues constantly reveals, is stating a principle, not laying down legislation: He is looking beyond the artificial conventions to the simple facts. His infinite compassion for those who have found the facts too hard for them is as clear as His refusal to compromise His statement of the ideal to which those facts point.

The teaching that St Mark associates with this renewal of public ministry is similar in character to that in Q which is probably Galilean. The blessing of the children, the challenge to the wealthy youth, the warning against riches and the promise of reward, are illustrations of the Beatitudes: but the note of crisis in stressing the importance of personal decision has now become urgent. The Pharisees have shown themselves definitely hostile; His disciples are distracted by misunderstandings; the time grows short. Deeply impressive is the description in *v.* 32 of the group: "They were on the road to Jerusalem; Jesus was in front; they were bewildered, and as they followed they grew afraid"; and of His solemn warning of the passion and death that awaits Him.

In spite of it they were still blinded by the false glamour of His Messiahship, by visions of thrones and crowns. He will offer nothing but the sharing of His own cup and baptism—the cup of pain, the baptism in blood; this and the knowledge that greatness consists only in service and that by suffering life is ennobled and redeemed. Timaeus, the beggar at Jericho, was not the only blind man on the road. Faith for him as eventually for the disciples was the condition of restored sight.

(3) *Three Days in Jerusalem.* At Bethany and Bethphage Jesus, who had already manifested His acceptance of St Peter's confession, acted dramatically upon it. The disciples had been deaf to His predictions of the Cross and His lessons of service: Zechariah's prophecy of a Messiah peaceful and riding on an ass might enlighten them. That His entry was directly suggested by the prophet's vision seems indisputable.

Next day He again went into Jerusalem and on the way enacted another parable, of a fig-tree, similar to that in Lk. xiii. 6–9. It is perhaps likely that the story of the withering had grown out of the remembrance of His words. In any case the message is the same: Israel, so frequently compared to a tree, had failed to produce fruit, and its doom was sealed.

The Synoptic record ascribes to this day's visit the Cleansing of the Temple which the Fourth Gospel had narrated at a much earlier point of the Ministry. If it took place in this last week, it may well have been a chief ground for the arrest and condemnation of Jesus; for it attacked a source of income to the priests and might have created a breach of the peace and led to trouble with Pilate, whose massacre of Galileans in the Temple (Lk. xiii. 1) was a recent memory. But it is also possible that it actually occurred on a previous visit, that St Mark knew of it, but not recording any other ministry in Jerusalem placed it here.

Next day He again visited the city and was challenged by what seems to have been a representative body of religious leaders. The question raised in Galilee, alike by the suggestion that He is inspired by Beelzebub and by the demand for a sign, is now made explicit. What is His authority? and what its source? As before, He refuses a direct reply: let them use their own insight: what is their verdict in the case of John the Baptist? They had not dared to support John: they do not dare, in face of his popularity, to disavow him. Expediency bids them decline to decide. To men who refuse to answer honestly an honest question, Jesus will not declare Himself.

Yet in fact He answers by parable. The Wicked Husbandmen is of course the story of God's dealings with Israel His vineyard. The imagery was familiar; the claim for Himself as beloved son and heir is manifest.

To arrest Jesus at the time was impossible: the deputation, if such it was, withdrew, resolved upon His destruction.

They sent to Him a group of Pharisees and officers of Herod—the Galileans who had first rejected Him. What is His verdict upon the Roman oppression? With words of flattery for His fearlessness and sincerity, they asked a question to which any answer would be fatal. Will He give the patriotic reply and ground for an accusation of treason; or admit Caesar's rule and forfeit His claim as a national leader? He saw their trap, took the question literally, asked for a Roman coin, and bade them give to Caesar what belongs to him, and to God what is God's: there is no such alternative between human and divine obligation as they had suggested. They stood amazed.

Then came the Sadducees with a question about the resurrection which gains point if the raising of Lazarus (Jn. xi) had lately taken place. It is the sort of problem popular with superficial sceptics. Jesus in His reply goes to the heart of the matter: those who are in communion with God are alive eternally, but immortality is not a mere prolonging of earthly conditions, nor resurrection a reanimation of the physical body. Much as we may desire to picture to ourselves the life hereafter, we must remember that our experience is not sufficient to enable us to know or to describe it.

There followed the question of an honest Rabbi whose sincerity Jesus recognised and proclaimed. Then He himself raised in the form of a question the issue on which He had already spoken so often. "Son of David", a second Solomon, was the current conception of the

Messiah: yet David (to whom the scholarship of that day ascribed the composition of Psalm cx) called the Messiah Lord: surely then Son of David is a misleading and inadequate description. The subsequent warning and commendation illustrate the distinction that He is drawing: it is not ambition and prestige, but the love that gives to the uttermost that is the true greatness.

(4) *The Apocalyptic Discourse*. This, the longest utterance of Jesus recorded by St Mark, is on other grounds regarded as dependent upon a separate and perhaps later source. Its special form, which has parallels in the last part of Q and elsewhere, will be considered later (cf. p. 99): but many of its lessons have already been reported and there seems no strong reason for rejecting it. That Jesus foresaw the ruin of Jerusalem is shown in the parable of the Wicked Husbandmen and many other non-apocalyptic passages (cf. Q, pp. 175, 183 and explicitly Lk. xix. 41–4).

The use of Apocalyptic, as has already been noted, was frequent and familiar. Eastern speech was then and is still clothed in metaphors and figurative language; this is particularly the case in poetical or eloquent utterance. Such speech is unfamiliar to Western ears and is easily misunderstood either by being taken literally or set down as gross exaggeration. This often happens in the case of Apocalyptic. Its imagery is indeed common throughout the Old Testament, where warnings of disaster and exhortations to wise decision are often clothed in metaphors of violent physical catastrophe. Such language is almost inevitable in times when the future is insecure and men are shaken out of their complacent trust in worldly success. To interpret the "signs" or the "second coming" literally as events destined to happen on the material level is to vulgarise the whole meaning of Apocalyptic. Rather it would seem to be the natural mode for describing the overwhelming grandeur and urgency of the spiritual; the natural symbolism for the energy of God. Those who have learned to live dangerously will know its significance: those who need proof that in times of crisis such utterance is universal need only turn back to the newspapers of August 1914.

B. *The Passion*

(1) *The Betrayal.* St Mark's note that two days before the Passover the chief priests agreed on immediate action bears out the Johannine rather than the Marcan dating; for in St John the Last Supper and Arrest take place not on the day of the Paschal meal but on the previous evening. For Jesus the anointing by the woman in Simon's house is the prelude: Jn. xii. 1 places it four days earlier, but gives an almost identical account of it: there is no means of deciding which date is correct. There follow the account of Judas' offer to betray His Master at a convenient time—an offer which it is fanciful to ascribe to his desire to fulfil the predictions of Jesus or to force the Master to reveal His power—the preparation for the Last Supper, the announcement of Judas' treachery, and the institution of the Eucharist.

They go out to the Mount of Olives and Jesus warns St Peter of his desertion: He enters Gethsemane, bids the disciples wait, and goes forward with the three to His agony. Judas appears and He is arrested.

(2) *The Trial and Crucifixion.* St Luke's account of the trials is somewhat different from St Mark's, and is probably more accurate. Though there may well have been a preliminary enquiry that night, most of it must have been spent in the court of the house where St Peter thrice denied Him and amid the horse-play of the servants. At morning the Sanhedrin met, and the explicit charge of His claim to be Messiah was put forward. Jesus admitted it, replying with two familiar Messianic texts (Ps. cix. 1; Dan. vii. 13). His reply was condemned as blasphemy and He was taken under guard to Pilate, where the charge was represented as treason against Caesar. Pilate, perhaps to exasperate the Jews or to share his responsibility, or from genuine desire to act justly, sent Jesus to Herod, and on His return proposed to scourge and release Him. This being resisted, he took the prisoner out to the people and offered to set Him free in honour of the feast. The priests demanded Barabbas and excited the people to shouts of "Crucify him". Pilate then pronounced sentence.

St Mark, St Luke and St John give independent and characteristic accounts of the Crucifixion. St Mark emphasises the loneliness and horror of the tragedy; St Luke the pity and courage of the Sufferer; St John His love and triumph. The words from the Cross, as traditionally arranged and whatever their source, form a noble epitome of the ministry: in the most difficult of them (Mk. xv. 34) Jesus fulfils to the uttermost His life of sacrifice and His own repeated saying: "Whoso loseth His life finds it". Nowhere is He more manifestly divine than when He surrenders even His assurance of God.

The rending of the Temple curtain is an apt symbol of His accomplishment: by His death He has opened the way to God. The centurion's acknowledgment is the firstfruits of its effect.

(3) *The Resurrection.* That evening before the Paschal Sabbath by Pilate's permission the body was laid in the tomb. All the records agree that early on the morning after the Sabbath Mary Magdalene and other women came to the tomb and found the stone rolled from its entrance. St Mark describes the message of the young man in a white robe and the promise that they shall see Jesus in Galilee: St Luke gives the promise as given during the Galilean ministry: both notice the fear of the women, and St Mark's account is broken off there.

The remaining narratives and the formal list of appearances given by St Paul (1 Cor. xv. 1–11) are not easily harmonised. Their divergence has been used as an argument against their authenticity and to discredit the fact. In view of the early and official character of the Pauline list and of the crucial importance of the event we might certainly expect a stereotyped consistency. Variety may well reflect the primitive character of the evidence and, to some extent at least, both the confusion of the disciples and the difficulty of giving an exact description of such experiences. Obviously there is need to weigh each testimony carefully, especially as between the Galilean and the Jerusalemite traditions. Probably it is impossible either to construct a satisfactory composite narrative, or to decide which account is more authoritative. But the combination of varying details with emphatic agreement as to the fact is surely suggestive both of the mode and of the reality of communion with the risen Lord. In considering the whole matter we must remember that we are dealing with an unprecedented event coming to men who had been living through a time of extreme tension and bitter disappointment, and that these men were wholly transformed by it, passing as a consequence from cowardice into joy, from despair into conviction, from ambition into fellowship. Divergent as their testimony may be, these men were absolutely united as to the certainty of the fact, were prepared to stake their lives upon its truth, and by preaching it have changed the whole history of mankind. Through the centuries since that first Easter there has been a succession of men and women of outstanding integrity and intelligence who have shared the experience and repeated the testimony.

CHAPTER IV

THE TEACHING OF JESUS

This chapter supplements the outline of the ministry by setting out the chief teaching characteristic of its several phases. The general ideas underlying His teaching have already been stated in chap. I, § C, where Christ's concepts are briefly compared with those of His contemporaries.

For further study in addition to those already mentioned the following are useful:

A. C. Clutton-Brock, *What is the Kingdom of Heaven?*

T. R. Glover, *The Jesus of History.*

C. E. Raven, *Christ and Modern Education.*

INTRODUCTORY

The ministry of Jesus falls, as we have seen, into three distinct periods; and His teaching is easily divided into three corresponding phases. There is first the period of public preaching in the synagogues and to the people in general, preaching that centres upon the proclamation of God's kingdom and aims at infecting the hearers with an apprehension of the reality of the kingdom and an appreciation of its character and demands. The second period, following as a consequence but necessitated also by the hostility of the religious leaders, is occupied with the training of the disciples and with the method of instruction by parable: this has the twofold effect of sifting out the spiritually sensitive and of quickening the insight and deepening the experience of the disciples. It is combined with close intimacy for them with Jesus and with a definite mission. It culminates in St Peter's confession of the Messiah. The third, for which all the rest has been a preparation, is concerned with the revelation by word and deed of what Messiahship involves, with the stripping off of false ideas of material welfare, of kingly power and of religious prestige, and with the fostering of new standards of obedience, service and fellowship. It leads up to the climax of the Crucifixion and Resurrection by which alone its purpose is attained.

Each of the later phases of teaching, distinct and characteristic as it is, includes and supplements what has gone before: the three constitute a continuous series, an education in discipleship which has the effect of lifting ordinary Galileans, of humble station, of widely differing temperaments, and of no special intelligence or culture, to a fullness of power, and a capacity for fellowship wholly unprecedented and unique in its influence. The stages of the training, adjusted as they are to the circumstances of the ministry, are yet equally adjusted to the needs of the learners. If the purpose of education is the development of personalities, then the method of Jesus, as judged by its results, deserves close and careful study.

It is important to stress this aspect of His teaching because too often its phases have been regarded rather as disconnected episodes than as coherent elements in a single whole. The preaching of the kingdom has been supposed to be inconsistent with that of the Messiahship; the Sermon on the Mount has been contrasted with the parables and with the Apocalyptic; the different stages have been said to be due to changes in the outlook and consciousness of Jesus Himself. It is even suggested that He began His work as a peasant-prophet aiming only at a spiritual revival in Judaism; that hardened by opposition He broke away from this purpose and organised a Church of His own followers; and that finally He encouraged them to claim for Him the title of Messiah, a claim wholly different from His original message, and, as some would argue, a disastrous mistake.

The answer to such theories is that they are true neither to the evidence of the records nor to the results of the ministry. Q, whose whole contents seem to be limited to Galilee and which most scholars would accept as giving primitive teaching, emphasises in the story of the Temptation exactly the lessons which St Mark represents Jesus as striving to impart to His disciples before His passion; in its account of His earliest utterances it ascribes to Him an authority identical with, if less explicit than, that of the Messiahship; throughout its pages it records teaching and describes action essentially the same as that of the last phase. From first to last, though there is development in His presentation of His message, its content and character are the same. Furthermore, all recent study, and especially that of Jewish scholars, has made clear that the fundamental distinction between Jesus and Judaism is that His religion centres in a person, and draws its power from the unique quality of His own personality. Authority, the authority of One who is conscious of His own relationship with God, is as typical of Q as of St Mark and of the public ministry as of the passion. Whatever change exists is due to the teacher's adjustment of His message to the growing capabilities of His pupils: it is His progressive unfolding to them of a single and coherent lesson. Characteristic of this combination of fundamental unity with developing presentation is the use of the title "Son of man", which Jesus applies to Himself from first to last at least eighty times in the Gospels. In the Old Testament the phrase had three familiar usages; in the Psalms as equivalent to man in general, e.g. "what is man...or the son of man" (Ps. viii. 4); in Ezekiel as the prophet's title when receiving the word of the Lord (cf. Ez. ii. 1, etc.) and therefore as signifying the representative of man before God; in Dan. vii. 13 "one like a son of man came with the clouds of heaven", and so more plainly in the book of Enoch, as signifying the glorified messenger of God to men. In the ministry of Jesus the significance of the title carries all three meanings, but there is a definite movement from the first which is perhaps sufficient for Mk. ii. 10 and 28, to the second (e.g. Lk. vii. 34; Q, p. 170) and so to the third (e.g. Mk. viii. 31 and xiv. 62), a movement corresponding to the growing appreciation of His hearers.

With this introduction we may consider the three phases separately.

I. The Public Ministry: Proclaiming the Kingdom

The message of Jesus, as Q not less than St Mark shows, follows upon that of John the Baptist, and is expressed in a similar phrase: "Repent, for the kingdom of heaven is at hand". Yet the meaning which the two attach to the words differs widely. To John repentance is essentially a renunciation of sin in face of the wrath to come: his teaching as given in L is negative in its emphasis: it takes up and applies the prohibitions and warnings of the old dispensation. To Jesus repentance is not only or chiefly renunciation of sin: it is the change of outlook and life which follows upon the experience of God: it is not a warning, but good news which men are invited to welcome and believe. The content of the good news and the meaning of God's kingdom are expressed in the Beatitudes and the section of Q which follows them. The kingdom is not to be identified with material welfare and success and popularity. These things, as Jesus had shown in His Temptation, are false ideals which blind and enslave. Love, generosity, fellowship, not for the sake of expected reward, but because such qualities are divine;

sympathy not criticism, pity not scorn, are the true fruit of religion. It is by conduct that character is known; the love of man is the necessary accompaniment of the love of God.

It is thus the nature of God that determines the right behaviour of men: if He is Father, then His children must be like Him; and conversely if their way of life is selfish, exclusive, ambitious, then their idea of God and their relation to Him are wrong. To accept God's kingdom is not merely to say "Lord, Lord"; it is to express the true nature of God in our words and deeds; it is to become akin to and sons of God.

The enlargement of the Sermon in M illustrates this by comparing the old law with the new gospel. Of old religion was mainly expressed in prohibitions: God is giver of the Law, and has forbidden certain evils. As Jesus proclaims it, it is not negative but positive: we are to be perfect because God is perfect, loving because He is Father of us all. Conduct thus springs from and expresses religion; morality is based not upon duty only but upon religious experience; the man who loves God will naturally live in love and sympathy with his fellows. To describe such teaching as concerned with behaviour rather than with faith and religion is to mistake its whole significance. For Jesus morality is the outward sign of religion, and religion the living source of right conduct.

The personality of Jesus gave power to His message. He impressed His hearers by the manifest fact that He was speaking not from books but from His own experience, not at second-hand but with direct knowledge. They recognised that He was Himself vividly and immediately conscious of God and could describe the character of the kingdom because He was within it. The incident of the centurion's servant illustrates this recognition of His "authority", and when John the Baptist questioned it He replied by appealing to the evidence of it.

It is this independence and creative originality of Jesus that brought Him into collision with the authorities. From the first He realised and in His earliest parables (Mk. ii. 21–2) expressed the hopelessness of the attempt to combine His way with theirs. The Law is an old robe, already beginning to wear out: to patch on to it a conflicting element (the "patch" is the freedom from the rule of fasting) is to hasten its destruction. The new message cannot be contained within the outward forms, the old wine-skins, that contained the old: new expression must be found for it. The contrast between the Law and the Gospel is not an invention of St Paul's.

Teaching of a similar character is found in many of the later sections of Q (e.g. pp. 175–8) and in the brief account of the public ministry in Judaea in Mk. x. There is the same stress upon God as contrasted with Mammon, upon vision and sensitiveness, sincerity and simplicity; the same contrast between the sophisticated selfishness of the worldly and the spontaneous friendliness of the kingdom; the same use of aphorism, the same vivid insight, the same poetry of thought and phrase. More than any human utterances these sayings carry a recognisable hall-mark: after nineteen centuries they still ring out fresh and arresting.

Their quality is more easily recognised than described. To call them "mystic" is to give an impression of vagueness or of abstraction: they are on the contrary clear-cut and concrete. Yet the true mysticism, which is the experience of union with God and therefore of intimate communion with His world and immediate perception of its significance, is the source from which they spring. Their beauty, their truth, their moral insight should be, and have been, infectious. This indeed is their purpose, that from them men should catch the spirit of the kingdom and find themselves native to it. Jesus does not argue them into belief, nor sway them by emotion, nor exhort in the manner of the moralist: He flings down phrases that illuminate like flashes of lightning; and sometimes the blind receive sight.

II. The Training of the Disciples: Teaching by Parables

A. *Lessons of Awareness of God*

The new phase begun by the appointment of the Twelve is signalised by a parable descriptive of His work hitherto. He has been sowing seeds of life, the word of good news, sowing it at random over the little field of His world. Some of it lies on hard ground; the Pharisees had proved themselves unresponsive: some is seized by the birds; their taunts had killed the faith of many: with some there is growth; but weeds of ambition and the scorching heat of criticism destroy it: some strikes root in a receptive soil; from it will come the harvest. Such is His explanation of the story: such has been the growth of the kingdom: His work is as simple and natural as husbandry.

To emphasise the naturalness of His religion, He

followed the one parable with another. Once the seed is sown, growth proceeds spontaneously; the farmer sleeps and wakes, the seed germinates in secret, and without further labour the soil produces blade and ear and corn. Here again it is His own method: these disciples must be free to grow: He will not restrain or coerce them: God's world is fitted to bring the crop to perfection: then He will put in the sickle.

These two parables might seem to minimise the hearer's responsibility: a third adjusts the imagery (Mk. iv. 21–2; cf. Q, p. 176). Mankind is not impassive like the soil. Rather is the message of the kingdom a lamp which men may cover up and hide away or set up on its stand: it is for them to let the light shine before men. At present it is secret, some day it will be revealed.

These three parables deal with the growth of the kingdom in the individual: its corporate aspect is more evident in the stories of the mustard-seed (Mk. iv. 31–2; Q, p. 182) and of the leaven (Q only) which emphasise the growth of the kingdom as a tree in which mankind can find rest and as the influence by which it will be transformed.

The other parables which apparently belong to this phase of the teaching are in M. Two, the Treasure-seeker and the Merchant, emphasise the lesson of the lamp, and the absolute claim of the kingdom to man's entire devotion. Two, the Tares and the Drag-net, are rather parables of judgment in which the kingdom seems to be regarded as a mixed society of good and bad until the final separation. This is difficult to reconcile with the teaching of Jesus and has been supposed to reflect a later and ecclesiastical outlook in which the Church as an organised society is prominent. If it is genuine, the kingdom must not be taken as identical with field or net, but as illuminated by the whole story: at present it is not manifest who are within the kingdom; judge not; there comes a time when the "sons of the kingdom" will be sorted out.

The great parables in L (Lk. x–xviii) seem also to belong to this phase of the ministry. This section of St Luke, though traditionally described as the ministry in Peraea, contains hardly any notes of time or place; and it is almost certain that in it the evangelist records material (from Q and other sources) of which he did not know the occasion. The teaching given in it is markedly different from that which follows the confession of Messiahship: the Q sections probably belong to the Galilean period: the great parables are closely linked with the ideas emphasised in the public ministry and are appropriate to the training of the disciples during which Jesus "spake not without a parable" (Mk. iv. 34). It is best therefore to consider these stories here.

The four long ones all illustrate the central message of the kingdom. The Good Samaritan (Lk. x. 30–7), in which, as in the Sower, it is easy to recognise a symbol of Jesus Himself, explains the essential character of the "son of the kingdom", the mercy which knows no limits of race or circumstance: the figures of priest and Levite indicate the contrast between profession and practice which had become evident in the conflict over the Sabbath (Mk. iii. 1–6). The parables of the Lost Sheep and the Lost Coin (Lk. xv. 1–10) enforce the same lesson, but as their conclusions show apply it to God. It is our life's task to be as the Good Samaritan, because our Father also seeks to save that which is being lost. The Prodigal Son (Lk. xv. 11–32) enlarges this picture of God and reveals an essential element in our Lord's conception of Him. God will not coerce His children, nor prevent the younger son from going out from his home into the far country: He will not soften the wind to the shorn lamb, nor forbid the free exercise of choice. But His love does not change; and when the boy comes to himself and returns, his father meets him and makes him welcome. Thus the parable supplements that of the Lost Sheep and takes up the message to the paralytic (Mk. ii. 5). It is also like the Good Samaritan, a parable of universality; for the two sons seem clearly to represent Jew and Gentile. To urge that it presupposes the Gentile mission of St Paul, and is therefore of doubtful authenticity, is to ignore the fact that Jesus, even in the teaching recorded in M, always represents God as the Father who has no favourites (Mt. v. 45) and is good to the unthankful and evil (Q in Lk. vi. 35). It is, however, possible that here as in his version of the patch on the old garment (Mk. ii. 21 = Lk. v. 36), St Luke has edited the story so as to strengthen the reference to the Gentiles.

The pair of parables in chap. xvi, the Unjust Steward and Dives and Lazarus, deal with man's responsibility for a right use of his earthly life. They may perhaps belong to the later phase of the ministry when this thought becomes specially prominent, as in the parables of the Great Supper, the Pounds and the Ten Virgins. But the need for human effort has been an element in the teaching from the beginning; and the parables of the Treasure-seeker and the Merchant already emphasise it.

The Unjust Steward has been supposed to be difficult, because "his lord commended him for acting prudently"[1] and Jesus is therefore supposed to have condoned his fraud. In fact the purpose of the parable is not obscure. Jesus tells the tale of an unscrupulous and self-centred agent who nevertheless exercises real foresight and ingenuity. If this worldling for material ends can use such qualities, surely the "sons of light" with their much higher aim ought not to be less prudent. By careful use of their material resources they must create a true fellowship which will endure eternally.

To forestall any misunderstanding as to the kind of means which may be employed, Jesus not only insists upon the absolute difference between God and Mammon and the absolute worth of the moral law (xvi. 16–18), but adds the parable of Dives and Lazarus. The rich man has ignored his opportunities, and refused sympathy: his blindness is fatal: the poor man inherits the kingdom; the rich has rejected it. The reference to the resurrection strengthens the possibility that these stories belong to the last phase of the ministry.

Two shorter parables, the Rich Fool (Lk. xii. 16–21) and the Barren Fig-tree (xiii. 6–9), enforce a similar lesson. The latter has been already cited in connection with the incident in Mk. xi. 12–15 (cf. p. 71) and is obviously similar to the teaching of the test of fruits in Q.

---

[1] Much of the difficulty arises because the Authorised Version mistranslates the adverb: it is shrewdness and prudence, not wisdom, for which the steward is praised.

In view of its reference to God's treatment of Israel it may well have been spoken later, and perhaps at the time of the Wicked Husbandmen.

B. *Lessons of Service*

Most of the training of the disciples is rather by example and the influence of intimacy than by instruction: but the charge to them before their mission (Mk. vi. 7–11; Q, pp. 171–3) takes up the lessons of the parables. They are to go like the sower scattering the seed everywhere: they are not to make special preparation but to depend upon the generosity of their hosts: they are not to seek out suitable hearers but to give the message to whatever household they enter[1]; some will receive it, others will refuse; by his decision each decides his own fate; the choice involves an issue more grave than that which befell Sodom: Chorazin and Bethsaida have already proved themselves lost.

The dilemma which underlies the whole story of the ministry here becomes apparent: on the one hand is the supreme urgency of the alternative; acceptance or rejection of the message is literally a matter of life and death: on the other hand Jesus cannot constrain men to accept either by force or by flattery; He can only proclaim the gospel to them patiently and continuously, and leave the response to it in their own hands: and it seems that they will reject it. When the call "Thou art my Son, the beloved" had come to Him at His Baptism, He had

[1] Mt. x. 11 alone gives instruction to seek out a worthy host: this seems to contradict the meaning of Mk. and Q, and probably reflects the method of a later time.

known its vital significance: in His Temptation He had
refused to take any of the easy roads: but the decision
then made is costly; will it be effective?

C. *Lessons of Communion*

The result of the mission was reassuring. Jesus shared
the joy of His disciples. The wise and prudent at Capernaum might reject the counsel of God as they had rejected the witness of John. Yet to babes God has revealed
it. Such is the Father's will, as Jesus had Himself proclaimed in His Beatitudes. There follows the outburst of
intimate union (Q, p. 173). A complete revelation has
indeed been entrusted to the Son by His Father: only the
Father knows the true nature of His Son: the Father is
known only by the Son and by those to whom the Son is
willing to reveal Him. It is for God and with God that
He fulfils His mission. The invitation which follows in
Mt. xi. 28–30 may not belong here: but is so similar in
its poetic form to the other two stanzas that it is most
probably part of the same utterance.

It is appropriate that after such an experience Jesus
should have given to His disciples the Lord's Prayer.
Here as in the Beatitudes the two Gospels differ, St Luke
giving the shorter version in our text. Possibly the
prayer was not in Q and is preserved by L and M in-
dependently: probably it came from Q and has been
enlarged in M. Its sequence is a notable indication of the
mind of Jesus. The Father comes first: worship is man's
first task: then intercession for the coming of the kingdom, for the day's food, for forgiveness which we can

only ask as we ourselves forgive, and for deliverance from the final trial.

This prayer was apparently followed by the parables of the Importunate Friend (Lk. xi. 5–8) and the Father and his Children (Q, p.174), which like that of the Unjust Judge (Lk. xviii. 1–8) are lessons in persistence on the *a fortiori* principle used in the Unjust Steward—"If ye being evil . . . how much more shall the heavenly Father". Possibly the parable of the Pharisee and the Publican (Lk. xviii. 10–14) also belongs here. It expresses the very spirit of penitent adoration in its contrast with complacency. But this contrast and the scene of the story make it likely that it belongs to the later denunciations of hypocrisy.

With this prayer should surely be associated the parable of the Two Debtors (Mt. xviii. 21–35), which while also a story of judgment is an exposition of the clause "Forgive us our trespasses as we forgive". It is grouped with a discourse that includes the parable of the Lost Sheep and probably belongs to this stage of the ministry.

If this is the order of His training, He has led His disciples from awareness of God in the parables, and service to Him in their mission, on to Communion with Him in prayer. It is this vital intercourse with the Father that is the essence of the Gospel: it is this which is the significance of the kingdom—God in us and we in God.

There is one further step to be taken. They have seen the character of the Father in the words and works of Jesus: a more intimate and complete expression of His being has still to be discovered by them. A person is more than his words and works: a person will convey to us who are ourselves persons what no other means can express: if the disciples can see the Father in His Son, their concept of God and their relationship to Him will be deepened and intensified. Love, the only power that can transform, will then become possible; for the love of person for person is on a higher plane of intimacy than any other human experience. God in nature may call out awe; God in the moral law obedience: God in Christ will bring into union the two strongest elements in human nature, adoration and love. So on the road to Caesarea Jesus submits to them the crucial question, "Whom say ye that I am?"

III. THE REVELATION OF MESSIAHSHIP

The confession of Jesus as the Christ was indeed, as the saying in Mt. xvi. 18 (which is almost certainly late) truly indicates, the foundation of the new religion. The fire which Jesus had come to cast upon the earth was then kindled. His ministry of teaching had reached its climax. His work among the Galileans was done. He could make a further and perhaps final attempt to gather to Him the people of Jerusalem.

Messiah was the inevitable title for Him. It made fully explicit the twofold status of representative of man to God and representative of God to man, which His previous self-chosen name "Son of Man" was now seen to have implied. But, as His immediate warnings amply prove, Messiahship was liable to grave misunderstanding. It was entangled with ideas of political freedom or of supernatural deliverance, and had indeed become symbolic of the hopes which an oppressed people fostered and which found expression both in outbreaks of armed rebellion and in the revolutionary literature of the Apocalyptists. The disciples inevitably accepted it in its current meaning: to purify it of misconceptions and to give it a content in terms of service and of suffering was the characteristic task of the last phase of the ministry.

Jesus Himself, as His whole teaching demonstrates, conceived His mission as incompatible with worldly success ("blessed are ye when men shall hate you", Q, p. 165) or with coercion either by force or by sign from heaven. Whether from the first or later, He understood His Messiahship in terms of the Second Isaiah's vision of the Suffering Servant and of Zechariah's king "meek and riding upon an ass". Opposition made it plain that He would be called to fulfil a ministry of suffering, that Jerusalem which killed the prophets would not change. Yet Jerusalem must have its opportunity of decision. The good news must be proclaimed: He must offer Himself to His own, even if His own would not receive Him. Hence along with the task of transforming the outlook of His disciples there is the further task of bringing His work to its crisis by a deliberate challenge to Jewry at the Passover.

The dilemma which had always confronted Him thus took a more precise and urgent shape. The issue is imminent, and tremendous: a choice of life or death awaits Him and also, though they know it not, His judges. But at the same time He must convince His disciples that, however terrible the decision, He must be content if need be to be betrayed, and they must learn to see that true sovereignty is not in thrones and crowns but in the love which is faithful unto death.

These two notes, the note of His claim as God's suffering Messiah and the note of immediate and irrevocable decision, dominate the teaching of this last phase.

Even in His public utterances the claim is now openly avowed. Discipleship of the kingdom involves a relationship with Himself, an insight into His significance. Thus He challenges the rich young ruler who addressed Him as "Good Master" (Mk. x. 17–18): is the epithet a mere convention, or, since God alone is good, does it reveal recognition of His quality? He fulfills Zechariah's prediction and receives the Messianic welcome of the people (Mk. xi. 7–10). He delivers the parable of the Wicked Husbandmen (Mk. xii. 1–9; cf. p. 72). He insists that the Messianic Son of David is also David's Lord (Mk. xii. 35–8).

Alongside the Marcan parable of the Husbandmen should be set the Labourers in the Vineyard in M (Mt. xx. 1–16). Here also the Vineyard is Israel, the symbol of God's kingdom. To work in it, many, the Jews, have been summoned early: others are admitted later: others at the very close of the day: none who are willing to enter are excluded, and all receive the same reward. Whether or no the "steward" is Christ, at least the reference is manifestly to His invitation of publicans and sinners into the kingdom and His refusal to recognise the privileges and prior claims of the "righteous". It is the familiar lesson, enforced also in the subsequent parable of the Two Sons (xxi. 28–31), of the contrast between exclusiveness and universality, the orthodox and the outcaste: but in its direct allusion to Judaism and to the mission of Jesus it makes that lesson explicit.

The same lesson in more evidently Messianic form is given in the parables of the Great Supper (Lk. xiv. 16–24) and the Marriage Feast (Mt. xxii. 1–14), which probably represent two versions of the same story,[1] though M has added a separate parable, the Wedding Garment. The symbol of a banquet was very familiar in Apocalyptic predictions of the glories of the Messiah; and would be recognised as easily as the symbol of the vineyard. Jesus lays the same stress here upon the summons to the outcastes, but adds the lesson that the privileged have rejected His summons. The reference to His own ministry and status is as clear as in the parable of the Wicked Husbandmen.

In all these and more plainly still in the parable of the Ten Virgins (Mt. xxv. 1–13), along with the claim to Messiahship, is the note of urgency. The doors will soon be shut and those who are not ready to meet the bridegroom[2] will be unable to enter afterwards. The necessary lamp must be kept alight.[3] Watchfulness is essential in view of the nearness and suddenness of the crisis.

The parables of Pounds and Talents develop further this lesson of preparedness, and in this respect are not unlike that of the Unjust Steward. Each man is re-

[1] This is also the case in the similar pair: the Pounds (Lk. xix. 12–27) and the Talents (Mt. xxv. 14–30). In both pairs there is an element of rebellion and punishment appearing in one version, in M's Marriage Feast and in L's Pounds. It is, on the whole, more likely that these accounts are independent than that they are drawn from Q.

[2] For this symbol cf. Mk. ii. 19, 20.

[3] Cf. Lk. xii. 35–6.

sponsible for the use that he makes of his opportunities: he must profit by his earthly circumstances; for they give scope for the growth of the "good seed" entrusted to him. But these parables link up also with the predictions of His own departure which Jesus had been constantly repeating since St Peter's confession. The time is at hand when the bridegroom will be taken away: He had foreseen it from the first (Mk. ii. 20); now it is near. The nobleman will leave his servants, and will expect them to make full use of his wealth; for when he returns he will call them to account. In L the setting of the story may well be taken from the historical mission of Archelaus, eldest son of Herod the Great, to Rome in order to secure his title to kingship: in any case it suggests the contrast between the Messiah's departure and His return, and warns the disciples both of the length of His absence and of the power which He will exercise when He "comes again".

As the crisis at Jerusalem grew nearer, the references to departure and return became more frequent and more urgent. In the discourse in Mk. xiii they are given in definitely Apocalyptic form. As has been already shown, this particular type of language and imagery was not only familiar both in the Old Testament and in the Apocalypses but is singularly appropriate to intense spiritual experience. Jesus had Himself used it previously, as in the last section of Q where He is teaching the need for expectancy and decision. It is certainly an exaggeration to represent His whole ministry as dominated by the thought of a sudden and dramatic catastrophe in consequence of which His sovereignty will be proclaimed.

It is hardly less an exaggeration to deny the significance of the Apocalyptic element. By it He conveys in a technique thoroughly familiar to His hearers the lessons which He gave also in more direct statement and in parables. He has come to call men to Himself and into God's kingdom: on their response hangs their future destiny: if they reject Him, there will be disaster and the passing away of the old order in violence and woe: yet it will not be defeat for Him or for His disciples: through trial, however prolonged, by deliverance swift and unexpected, at an hour unknown even to Himself, God's kingdom will be established. Fearful results will follow the rejection which He sees to be coming; horrors of bloodshed and persecution will befall the world: for in rejecting Him mankind will have reinforced their own worldliness and rendered their "redemption" harder; and calamity is at once the inevitable consequence and the necessary remedy. But when their trust in godless standards and their pursuit of selfish aims bring their world crashing about them, there will come opportunity for a vision of the Son of Man in His glory. Such opportunity will in fact come in the lifetime of His hearers. Let them therefore be ready.

With this message, sure that the crisis is God's will, and that, though to the world He is being judged, yet really the position is reversed and He is judging His judges, He goes to His passion. The issues are tremendous, not for Him only, but for His people: failure will be supreme tragedy: yet the matter must be put to the test. Somehow, somewhen, God will vindicate Him, and bring in the kingdom: if all men fail Him, God stands sure.

On the last evening before His crucifixion He expressed the fullness of His teaching in an act in which Christians through the ages have found the supreme symbol and instrument of their Master. The Eucharist which He then instituted takes up the images of Corn and Vine used in the parables, and the familiar idea of the Messianic banquet: it is linked up with the festival of the Passover and the memories of Israel's deliverance from bondage: it marks out Jesus as the Offering by which God's deliverance is made effective: it renews the lesson of the oft-uttered words "Whoso loseth his life for my sake shall find it", which the Cross was to repeat next day: it completes the binding together of the disciples into a vital fellowship: it demonstrates that the new life of the kingdom consists in sharing in the life of Jesus, its King: it secures at once a perfect expression of communion with Him and a means by which that communion may be perpetually maintained and enlarged. Here as elsewhere it is impossible to determine how far all these elements were present at the time in the minds of the disciples or in the purpose of Jesus: the passage of centuries has emphasised now one, now another of them. But from the first it seems clear that the earliest Church found in this sacramental act a satisfying epitome of what they had learnt and believed, a satisfying means of expressing and developing their union with God, with Jesus and with one another.

CONCLUSION

Important as it is to study the teaching of Jesus during the period of His ministry, it is a mistake to separate His words from His deeds or from the influence of His death and resurrection. These are a vital part of His message, the events in which the teaching is summed up, expressed and made effective. We may summarise the results of His revelation under four heads.

I. He had given to Men an unique Revelation of God

Mankind, and especially the people of Israel, had been seeking after God, and "at sundry times and in divers manners" had found Him, in nature, in the moral law, in ceremonial observances, in the visions and experiences of the prophets, in the thought and learning of the wise. Gradually by these means their concept of God had been purified and enlarged, until in the noblest of their utterances they approach close to the teaching of Jesus. His work was not only to express what His forerunners had been groping after: if that had been all, He would have been no more than the chief of saints and prophets. Men found in Him something different, new and unique. Behind His words and acts, in the quality of His life and character, they realised the divine. Others had spoken of God and done God-like deeds: He showed them God, infected them with the sense of God's presence, fulfilled all their ideas of God, in His own person. So compelling was this conviction that it overcame all their prejudices, their fear of blasphemy and of idolatry, and compelled them to confess Him as their Lord. The resurrection taught them that communion with Him was not destroyed but strengthened by death; the Ascension made them sure that He was one with the Father. Henceforth God was for them in Christ: to live in Him, in His presence and Spirit, was to be at one with the eternal.

II. HE HAD DELIVERED MEN FROM SIN

In the life of Jesus they had seen power to overcome the world of sin and calamity. His teaching had shown them that sin was separation from God, that God desired and enabled men to repent, that by responding to God's unchanging love they could be set free from the dominion of evil. His works had revealed His authority over disease, His readiness to forgive, His compassion for sinners. His resurrection proved that He could bring good out of evil and turn defeat into victory: He had suffered the worst that the world could do against Him, a death of loneliness and shame, and by it He had attained a richer fullness of life. Moreover, as they learned from Him and caught something of His Spirit, they found themselves being released from the grip of temptation and filled with fresh power. He had saved them: He was the Saviour: in Him God was reconciling the world to Himself. The fight against evil was no longer a succession of efforts to overcome particular sins: rather their lives had found a new centre, and seeking to follow Christ they found themselves not only able to resist, but untouched by the desire to do wrong. Love for Him set them free from self, transformed them into His likeness, and enabled them to "fulfil the Law".

III. He had United them in the Fellowship of His Kingdom

Jesus had not only saved them from sin: He had saved them into brotherhood. The Kingdom of God had been His message from the first: it had been for centuries the dream that had fascinated Israel: it is an ideal that haunts even the loneliest and most worldly; for all human beings want love. Yet His disciples had not experienced the full fellowship of the Kingdom from His teaching. Even when they had confessed Him as Messiah, they were still tempted by ambition and jealousy. Not until they had forsaken Him and fled, and discovered their own helplessness, and been humbled to the dust, were they freed from the selfishness which destroys friendliness. Only after the resurrection and ascension was God's gift of fellowship received at Pentecost, when they became "of one heart and one mind", members one of another, in the society or body of Christ. As they realised more fully the glory of Jesus, they were more intimately united in trust and comradeship, each in all and all for each. The Church was no mere collection of professed believers, it was the blessed community whose life was the Spirit of Christ and whose business was the accomplishment of His will. Love united them to Him and so to one another.

IV. He had given them a World-wide and Life-long Work

Fellowship exists in the living of a shared life and the doing of a common task. The constant service of a great cause calls out the best in men and women. As they express their ideals in action, they discover fresh resources of energy. Jesus both by precept and example had trained His followers to "go and do likewise": He trusted them to hand on His message and complete His work: He commissioned them to go and make disciples of all nations. The very magnitude of the undertaking, so vast in proportion to their numbers and equipment, was an inspiration: for men rise to a great opportunity when they will ignore a small one. Assured that God was with them, freed from the fears and self-regard that foster cowardice and excuse evasion, confident in their loyalty to their Master and to one another, they set themselves dauntlessly to their grand adventure; and, as they engaged in it, day by day found strength to go forward.

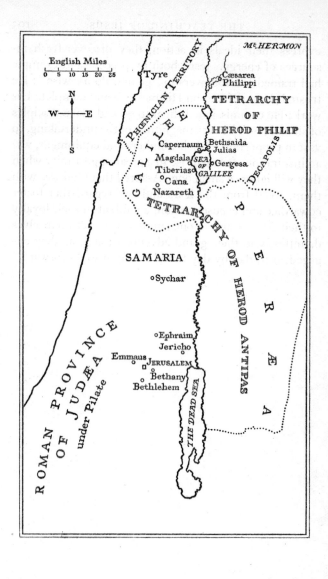

THE GOSPEL ACCORDING TO
ST MARK

✠

I. THE GOOD NEWS OF THE KINGDOM AND THE RESULTING CONFLICT

A. The Beginning

1. THE FORERUNNER

1 The beginning of the gospel of Jesus Christ, the Son of 1
God.

Even as it is written in Isaiah the prophet,[1]   2
Behold, I send my messenger before thy face,
Who shall prepare thy way;
The voice of one crying in the wilderness,   3
Make ye ready the way of the Lord,
Make his paths straight;

John came, who baptized in the wilderness and preached 4
the baptism of repentance unto remission of sins.[2] And 5
there went out unto him all the country of Judæa, and
all they of Jerusalem; and they were baptized of him in
the river Jordan, confessing their sins. And John was 6
clothed with camel's hair, and had a leathern girdle about
his loins, and did eat locusts and wild honey. And he 7
preached, saying, There cometh after me he that is
mightier than I, the latchet of whose shoes I am not
worthy to stoop down and unloose. I baptized you with 8
water; but he shall baptize you with the Holy Ghost.

---

[1] The quotation is from Malachi iii. 1 and Isaiah xl. 3.
[2] Cf. p. 84.

2. THE CALL
(for this section cf. Q, pp. 163–5 and pp. 52–3)

9   And it came to pass in those days, that Jesus came from Nazareth of Galilee, and was baptized of John in the
10   Jordan. And straightway coming up out of the water, he saw the heavens rent asunder, and the Spirit as a dove
11   descending upon him: and a voice came out of the heavens, Thou art my beloved Son, in thee I am well pleased.

12   And straightway the Spirit driveth him forth into the
13   wilderness. And he was in the wilderness forty days tempted of Satan; and he was with the wild beasts; and the angels[1] ministered unto him.

14   Now after that John was delivered up,[2] Jesus came
15   into Galilee, preaching the gospel of God, and saying, The time is fulfilled, and the kingdom of God is at hand: repent ye, and believe in the gospel.

16   And passing along by the sea of Galilee, he saw Simon and Andrew the brother of Simon casting a net in the
17   sea: for they were fishers. And Jesus said unto them, Come ye after me, and I will make you to become fishers
18   of men. And straightway they left the nets, and followed
19   him. And going on a little further, he saw James the son of Zebedee, and John his brother, who also were in the
20   boat mending the nets. And straightway he called them: and they left their father Zebedee in the boat with the hired servants, and went after him.

[1] Cf. p. 29.   [2] Cf. pp. 53–4.

3. A SABBATH IN CAPERNAUM
(cf. p. 54)

And they go into Capernaum; and straightway on the 21
sabbath day he entered into the synagogue[1] and taught.
And they were astonished at his teaching: for he taught 22
them as having authority, and not as the scribes.[2] And 23
straightway there was in their synagogue a man with an
unclean spirit;[3] and he cried out, saying, What have we 24
to do with thee, thou Jesus of Nazareth? art thou come
to destroy us? I know thee who thou art, the Holy One
of God. And Jesus rebuked him, saying, Hold thy peace, 25
and come out of him. And the unclean spirit, tearing him 26
and crying with a loud voice, came out of him. And they 27
were all amazed, insomuch that they questioned among
themselves, saying, What is this? a new teaching! with
authority he commandeth even the unclean spirits, and
they obey him. And the report of him went out straight- 28
way everywhere into all the region of Galilee round
about.

And straightway, when they were come out of the 29
synagogue, they came into the house of Simon and
Andrew, with James and John. Now Simon's wife's 30
mother lay sick of a fever; and straightway they tell him
of her: and he came and took her by the hand, and raised 31
her up; and the fever left her, and she ministered unto
them.

And at even, when the sun did set, they brought unto 32
him all that were sick, and them that were possessed with
devils. And all the city was gathered together at the door. 33

[1] Cf. pp. 14, 15.   [2] Cf. p. 14.   [3] Cf. pp. 28–30.

34 And he healed many that were sick with divers diseases, and cast out many devils; and he suffered not the devils to speak, because they knew him.

B. Growing Hostility

1. THE FIRST JOURNEYING

35 And in the morning, a great while before day, he rose up and went out, and departed into a desert place, and
36 there prayed. And Simon and they that were with him
37 followed after him; and they found him, and say unto
38 him, All are seeking thee. And he saith unto them, Let us go elsewhere into the next towns, that I may preach
39 there also; for to this end came I forth.[1] And he went into their synagogues throughout all Galilee, preaching and casting out devils.

40 And there cometh to him a leper, beseeching him, and kneeling down to him, and saying unto him, If thou wilt,
41 thou canst make me clean. And being moved with compassion, he stretched forth his hand, and touched him,
42 and saith unto him, I will; be thou made clean. And straightway the leprosy departed from him, and he was
43 made clean. And he strictly charged him, and straight-
44 way sent him out, and saith unto him, See thou say nothing to any man: but go thy way, shew thyself to the priest, and offer for thy cleansing the things which Moses
45 commanded, for a testimony unto them. But he went out, and began to publish it much, and to spread abroad the matter, insomuch that Jesus could no more openly

[1] Cf. p. 53.

enter into a city, but was without in desert places: and they came to him from every quarter.

2. THE GROWTH OF SUSPICION
(cf. pp. 55–6)

2 And when he entered again into Capernaum after some 1 days, it was noised that he was in the house. And many 2 were gathered together, so that there was no longer room for them, no, not even about the door: and he spake the word unto them. And they come, bringing unto him a 3 man sick of the palsy, borne of four. And when they 4 could not come nigh unto him for the crowd, they uncovered the roof where he was: and when they had broken it up, they let down the bed whereon the sick of the palsy lay. And Jesus seeing their faith saith unto the sick of the 5 palsy, Son, thy sins are forgiven.[1] But there were certain 6 of the scribes sitting there, and reasoning in their hearts, Why doth this man thus speak? he blasphemeth: who 7 can forgive sins but one, even God? And straightway 8 Jesus, perceiving in his spirit that they so reasoned within themselves, saith unto them, Why reason ye these things in your hearts? Whether is easier, to say to the 9 sick of the palsy, Thy sins are forgiven; or to say, Arise, and take up thy bed, and walk? But that ye may know 10 that the Son of man[2] hath power on earth to forgive sins (he saith to the sick of the palsy), I say unto thee, Arise, 11 take up thy bed, and go unto thy house. And he arose, 12 and straightway took up the bed, and went forth before them all; insomuch that they were all amazed, and glorified God, saying, We never saw it on this fashion.

[1] Cf. pp. 23, 55.   [2] Cf. pp. 83–4.

13 And he went forth again by the sea side; and all the
14 multitude resorted unto him, and he taught them. And
as he passed by, he saw Levi the son of Alphæus sitting
at the place of toll, and he saith unto him, Follow me.
15 And he arose and followed him. And it came to pass, that
he was sitting at meat in his house, and many publicans[1]
and sinners[2] sat down with Jesus and his disciples: for
16 there were many, and they followed him. And the scribes
of the Pharisees,[3] when they saw that he was eating with
the sinners and publicans, said unto his disciples, He
17 eateth and drinketh with publicans and sinners. And
when Jesus heard it, he saith unto them, They that are
whole have no need of a physician, but they that are sick:
I came not to call the righteous, but sinners.

18 And John's disciples and the Pharisees were fasting:
and they come and say unto him, Why do John's disciples
and the disciples of the Pharisees fast, but thy disciples
19 fast not? And Jesus said unto them, Can the sons of the
bride-chamber fast, while the bridegroom is with them?[4]
as long as they have the bridegroom with them, they
20 cannot fast. But the days will come, when the bridegroom shall be taken away from them, and then will they
21 fast in that day. No man seweth a piece of undressed
cloth on an old garment: else that which should fill it up
taketh from it, the new from the old, and a worse rent is
22 made. And no man putteth new wine into old wine-
skins: else the wine will burst the skins, and the wine
perisheth, and the skins: but they put new wine into
fresh wine-skins.[5]

---

[1] Cf. p. 11.   [2] Cf. p. 21.   [3] Cf. pp. 19, 20.
[4] Cf. pp. 28, 98 and Jn. iii. 29.   [5] Cf. p. 86.

And it came to pass, that he was going on the sabbath 23
day through the cornfields; and his disciples began, as
they went, to pluck the ears of corn. And the Pharisees 24
said unto him, Behold, why do they on the sabbath day
that which is not lawful? And he said unto them, Did ye 25
never read what David did,[1] when he had need, and was
an hungred, he, and they that were with him? How he 26
entered into the house of God when Abiathar was high
priest, and did eat the shewbread, which it is not lawful to
eat save for the priests, and gave also to them that were
with him? And he said unto them, The sabbath was made 27
for man, and not man for the sabbath: so that the Son of 28
man is lord even of the sabbath.

3. THE BREACH WITH THE LOCAL AUTHORITIES

3 And he entered again into the synagogue; and there was 1
a man there which had his hand withered. And they 2
watched him, whether he would heal him on the sabbath
day; that they might accuse him. And he saith unto the 3
man that had his hand withered, Stand forth. And he 4
saith unto them, Is it lawful on the sabbath day to do
good, or to do harm? to save a life, or to kill? But they
held their peace. And when he had looked round about 5
on them with anger, being grieved at the hardening of
their heart, he saith unto the man, Stretch forth thy hand.
And he stretched it forth: and his hand was restored.

---

[1] Cf. 1 Sam. xxi. 1–6 where the high priest is Ahimelech not
Abiathar, his son and successor.

6 And the Pharisees went out, and straightway with the Herodians[1] took counsel against him, how they might destroy him.

II. THE TRAINING OF THE DISCIPLES

A. THE APPOINTMENT OF THE TWELVE
(cf. pp. 56–7)

7 And Jesus with his disciples withdrew to the sea: and a great multitude from Galilee followed: and from Judæa,
8 and from Jerusalem, and from Idumæa, and beyond Jordan, and about Tyre and Sidon, a great multitude,
9 hearing what great things he did, came unto him. And he spake to his disciples, that a little boat should wait on him because of the crowd, lest they should throng him:
10 for he had healed many; insomuch that as many as had plagues pressed upon him that they might touch him.
11 And the unclean spirits, whensoever they beheld him, fell down before him, and cried, saying, Thou art the
12 Son of God. And he charged them much that they should not make him known.

13 And he goeth up into the mountain, and calleth unto him whom he himself would: and they went unto him.
14 And he appointed twelve,[2] that they might be with him,
15 and that he might send them forth to preach, and to have
16 authority to cast out devils:[3] and Simon he surnamed
17 Peter; and James the son of Zebedee, and John the

[1] Cf. p. 18.
[2] For other lists cf. Mt. x. 3; Lk. vi. 14; Acts i. 13.
[3] Cf. Mk. vi. 7.

brother of James; and them he surnamed Boanerges,[1]
which is, Sons of thunder: and Andrew, and Philip, and 18
Bartholomew, and Matthew, and Thomas, and James
the son of Alphæus, and Thaddæus, and Simon the
Cananæan,[2] and Judas Iscariot, which also betrayed him. 19

And he cometh into a house. And the multitude 20
cometh together again, so that they could not so much as
eat bread. And when his friends heard it, they went out 21
to lay hold on him: for they said, He is beside himself.
And the scribes which came down from Jerusalem said, 22
He hath Beelzebub, and, By the prince of the devils
casteth he out the devils. And he called them unto him, 23
and said unto them in parables, How can Satan cast out
Satan? And if a kingdom be divided against itself, that 24
kingdom cannot stand. And if a house be divided against 25
itself, that house will not be able to stand. And if Satan 26
hath risen up against himself, and is divided, he cannot
stand, but hath an end. But no one can enter into the 27
house of the strong man, and spoil his goods, except he
first bind the strong man; and then he will spoil his
house.[3] Verily I say unto you, All their sins shall be 28
forgiven unto the sons of men, and their blasphemies
wherewith soever they shall blaspheme: but whosoever 29
shall blaspheme against the Holy Spirit hath never forgiveness, but is guilty of an eternal sin:[4] because they 30
said, He hath an unclean spirit.

And there come his mother and his brethren; and, 31
standing without, they sent unto him, calling him. And 32
a multitude was sitting about him; and they say unto

---

[1] Cf. pp. 37–8.   [2] Cf. p. 21.
[3] Cf. Q, p. 175; Lk. xi. 21.   [4] Cf. Q, p. 179; Lk. xii. 10.

him, Behold, thy mother and thy brethren without seek
33 for thee. And he answereth them, and saith, Who is my
34 mother and my brethren? And looking round on them
which sat round about him, he saith, Behold, my mother
35 and my brethren! For whosoever shall do the will of
God, the same is my brother, and sister, and mother.

B. Their Teaching by Word and Example

1. PARABLES OF THE GROWTH OF THE KINGDOM (cf. pp. 58, 87–8)

4 1 And again he began to teach by the sea side. And there
is gathered unto him a very great multitude, so that he
entered into a boat, and sat in the sea; and all the multi-
2 tude were by the sea on the land. And he taught them
many things in parables, and said unto them in his
3 teaching, Hearken: Behold, the sower went forth to sow:
4 and it came to pass, as he sowed, some seed fell by the
5 way side, and the birds came and devoured it. And other
fell on the rocky ground, where it had not much earth;
and straightway it sprang up, because it had no deepness
6 of earth: and when the sun was risen, it was scorched;
7 and because it had no root, it withered away. And other
fell among the thorns, and the thorns grew up, and
8 choked it, and it yielded no fruit. And others fell into
the good ground, and yielded fruit, growing up and in-
creasing; and brought forth, thirtyfold, and sixtyfold,
9 and a hundredfold. And he said, Who hath ears to hear,
let him hear.

10   And when he was alone, they that were about him with

the twelve asked of him the parables. And he said unto 11 them, Unto you is given the mystery of the kingdom of God: but unto them that are without, all things are done in parables: that seeing they may see, and not perceive; 12 and hearing they may hear, and not understand; lest haply they should turn again, and it should be forgiven them. And he saith unto them, Know ye not this parable? 13 and how shall ye know all the parables? The sower soweth 14 the word. And these are they by the way side, where the 15 word is sown; and when they have heard, straightway cometh Satan, and taketh away the word which hath been sown in them. And these in like manner are they that are 16 sown upon the rocky places, who, when they have heard the word, straightway receive it with joy; and they have 17 no root in themselves, but endure for a while; then, when tribulation or persecution ariseth because of the word, straightway they stumble. And others are they that are 18 sown among the thorns; these are they that have heard the word, and the cares of the world, and the deceitfulness 19 of riches, and the lusts of other things entering in, choke the word, and it becometh unfruitful. And those are they 20 that were sown upon the good ground; such as hear the word, and accept it, and bear fruit, thirtyfold, and sixty-fold, and a hundredfold.

And he said unto them, Is the lamp brought to be put 21 under the bushel, or under the bed, and not to be put on the stand? For there is nothing hid, save that it should be 22 manifested; neither was anything made secret, but that it should come to light. If any man hath ears to hear, let 23 him hear. And he said unto them, Take heed what ye 24 hear: with what measure ye mete it shall be measured

25 unto you: and more shall be given unto you. For he that
hath, to him shall be given: and he that hath not, from
him shall be taken away even that which he hath.

26 And he said, So is the kingdom of God, as if a man
27 should cast seed upon the earth; and should sleep and
rise night and day, and the seed should spring up and
28 grow, he knoweth not how. The earth beareth fruit of
herself; first the blade, then the ear, then the full corn in
29 the ear. But when the fruit is ripe, straightway he putteth
forth the sickle, because the harvest is come.[1]

30 And he said, How shall we liken the kingdom of God?
31 or in what parable shall we set it forth? It is like a grain
of mustard seed, which, when it is sown upon the earth,
though it be less than all the seeds that are upon the earth,
32 yet when it is sown, groweth up, and becometh greater
than all the herbs, and putteth out great branches; so that
the birds of the heaven can lodge under the shadow
thereof.

33 And with many such parables spake he the word unto
34 them, as they were able to hear it: and without a parable
spake he not unto them: but privately to his own disciples
he expounded all things.

2. WORKS OF POWER
(cf. pp. 58–61)

35 And on that day, when even was come, he saith unto
36 them, Let us go over unto the other side. And leaving
the multitude, they take him with them, even as he was,
37 in the boat. And other boats were with him. And there
ariseth a great storm of wind, and the waves beat into the

[1] This parable is only found here.

boat, insomuch that the boat was now filling. And he 38
himself was in the stern, asleep on the cushion: and they
awake him, and say unto him, Master, carest thou not
that we perish? And he awoke, and rebuked the wind, 39
and said unto the sea, Peace, be still. And the wind
ceased, and there was a great calm. And he said unto 40
them, Why are ye fearful? have ye not yet faith? And 41
they feared exceedingly, and said one to another, Who
then is this, that even the wind and the sea obey him?

5 And they came to the other side of the sea, into the country 1
of the Gerasenes. And when he was come out of the boat, 2
straightway there met him out of the tombs a man with
an unclean spirit, who had his dwelling in the tombs: and 3
no man could any more bind him, no, not with a chain;
because that he had been often bound with fetters and 4
chains, and the chains had been rent asunder by him,
and the fetters broken in pieces: and no man had strength
to tame him. And always, night and day, in the tombs 5
and in the mountains, he was crying out, and cutting
himself with stones. And when he saw Jesus from afar, 6
he ran and worshipped him; and crying out with a loud 7
voice, he saith, What have I to do with thee, Jesus, thou
Son of the Most High God? I adjure thee by God, torment me not. For he said unto him, Come forth, thou 8
unclean spirit, out of the man. And he asked him, What 9
is thy name? And he saith unto him, My name is Legion;
for we are many. And he besought him much that he 10
would not send them away out of the country. Now there 11
was there on the mountain side a great herd of swine
feeding. And they besought him, saying, Send us into 12
the swine, that we may enter into them. And he gave 13

them leave. And the unclean spirits came out, and entered into the swine: and the herd rushed down the steep into the sea, in number about two thousand; and

14 they were choked in the sea. And they that fed them fled, and told it in the city, and in the country. And they came

15 to see what it was that had come to pass. And they come to Jesus, and behold him that was possessed with devils sitting, clothed and in his right mind, even him that had

16 the legion: and they were afraid. And they that saw it declared unto them how it befell him that was possessed

17 with devils, and concerning the swine. And they began

18 to beseech him to depart from their borders. And as he was entering into the boat, he that had been possessed with devils besought him that he might be with him.

19 And he suffered him not, but saith unto him, Go to thy house unto thy friends, and tell them how great things the Lord hath done for thee, and how he had mercy on

20 thee. And he went his way, and began to publish in Decapolis how great things Jesus had done for him: and all men did marvel.

21 And when Jesus had crossed over again in the boat unto the other side, a great multitude was gathered unto

22 him: and he was by the sea. And there cometh one of the rulers of the synagogue, Jaïrus by name; and seeing him,

23 he falleth at his feet, and beseecheth him much, saying, My little daughter is at the point of death: I pray thee, that thou come and lay thy hands on her, that she may be

24 made whole, and live. And he went with him; and a great multitude followed him, and they thronged him.

25 And a woman, which had an issue of blood twelve

26 years, and had suffered many things of many physicians,

and had spent all that she had, and was nothing bettered, but rather grew worse, having heard the things con- 27 cerning Jesus, came in the crowd behind, and touched his garment. For she said, If I touch but his garments, 28 I shall be made whole. And straightway the fountain of 29 her blood was dried up; and she felt in her body that she was healed of her plague. And straightway Jesus, per- 30 ceiving in himself that the power proceeding from him had gone forth, turned him about in the crowd, and said, Who touched my garments? And his disciples said unto 31 him, Thou seest the multitude thronging thee, and sayest thou, Who touched me? And he looked round about to 32 see her that had done this thing. But the woman fearing 33 and trembling, knowing what had been done to her, came and fell down before him, and told him all the truth. And he said unto her, Daughter, thy faith hath made thee 34 whole; go in peace, and be whole of thy plague.

While he yet spake, they come from the ruler of the 35 synagogue's house, saying, Thy daughter is dead: why troublest thou the Master any further? But Jesus, not 36 heeding the word spoken, saith unto the ruler of the synagogue, Fear not, only believe. And he suffered no 37 man to follow with him, save Peter, and James, and John the brother of James. And they come to the house of the 38 ruler of the synagogue; and he beholdeth a tumult, and many weeping and wailing greatly. And when he was 39 entered in, he saith unto them, Why make ye a tumult, and weep? the child is not dead, but sleepeth. And they 40 laughed him to scorn. But he, having put them all forth, taketh the father of the child and her mother and them that were with him, and goeth in where the child was.

41 And taking the child by the hand, he saith unto her,
Talitha cumi; which is, being interpreted, Damsel, I say
42 unto thee, Arise. And straightway the damsel rose up,
and walked; for she was twelve years old. And they were
43 amazed straightway with a great amazement. And he
charged them much that no man should know this: and
he commanded that something should be given her to
eat.

6 1 And he went out from thence; and he cometh into his
2 own country; and his disciples follow him. And when
the sabbath was come, he began to teach in the synagogue:
and many hearing him were astonished, saying, Whence
hath this man these things? and, What is the wisdom that
is given unto this man, and what mean such mighty works
3 wrought by his hands? Is not this the carpenter, the son
of Mary, and brother of James, and Joses, and Judas,
and Simon? and are not his sisters here with us? And
4 they were offended in him. And Jesus said unto them,
A prophet is not without honour, save in his own
country, and among his own kin, and in his own house.
5 And he could there do no mighty work, save that he laid
6 his hands upon a few sick folk, and healed them. And
he marvelled because of their unbelief.

And he went round about the villages teaching.

C. By Practice and Experience

1. THE MISSION AND ITS LESSON OF POWER
(cf. pp. 61–2)

7   And he called unto him the twelve, and began to send
them forth by two and two; and he gave them authority

over the unclean spirits; and he charged them that they 8
should take nothing for their journey, save a staff only;
no bread, no wallet, no money in their purse; but to go 9
shod with sandals: and, said he, put not on two coats.
And he said unto them, Wheresoever ye enter into a 10
house, there abide till ye depart thence. And whatsoever 11
place shall not receive you, and they hear you not, as ye
go forth thence, shake off the dust that is under your feet
for a testimony unto them. And they went out, and 12
preached that men should repent. And they cast out 13
many devils, and anointed with oil many that were sick,
and healed them.

[INTERLUDE—THE FATE OF JOHN]

And king Herod[1] heard thereof; for his name had 14
become known: and he said, John the Baptist is risen
from the dead, and therefore do these powers work in
him. But others said, It is Elijah. And others said, It is 15
a prophet, even as one of the prophets. But Herod, when 16
he heard thereof, said, John, whom I beheaded, he is
risen. For Herod himself had sent forth and laid hold 17
upon John, and bound him in prison for the sake of
Herodias, his brother Philip's wife:[2] for he had married
her. For John said unto Herod, It is not lawful for thee 18
to have thy brother's wife. And Herodias set herself 19
against him, and desired to kill him; and she could not;
for Herod feared John, knowing that he was a righteous 20
man and a holy, and kept him safe. And when he heard
him, he was much perplexed; and he heard him gladly.

[1] Cf. p. 11.
[2] Not Philip the Tetrarch but a half-brother who lived in Rome.

21 And when a convenient day was come, that Herod on his birthday made a supper to his lords, and the high cap-
22 tains, and the chief men of Galilee; and when the daughter of Herodias[1] herself came in and danced, she pleased Herod and them that sat at meat with him; and the king said unto the damsel, Ask of me whatsoever thou wilt,
23 and I will give it thee. And he sware unto her, What-soever thou shalt ask of me, I will give it thee, unto the
24 half of my kingdom. And she went out, and said unto her mother, What shall I ask? And she said, The head
25 of John the Baptist. And she came in straightway with haste unto the king, and asked, saying, I will that thou forthwith give me in a charger the head of John the
26 Baptist. And the king was exceeding sorry; but for the sake of his oaths, and of them that sat at meat, he would
27 not reject her. And straightway the king sent forth a soldier of his guard, and commanded to bring his head:
28 and he went and beheaded him in the prison, and brought his head in a charger, and gave it to the damsel; and the
29 damsel gave it to her mother. And when his disciples heard thereof, they came and took up his corpse, and laid it in a tomb.

2. EVIDENCES OF POWER
(cf. pp. 62–4: and Jn. vi. 1–21)

30 And the apostles gather themselves together unto Jesus; and they told him all things, whatsoever they had
31 done, and whatsoever they had taught. And he saith unto them, Come ye yourselves apart into a desert place,

[1] If this reading is correct, Salome afterwards wife of Philip the Tetrarch is meant.

and rest a while. For there were many coming and going, and they had no leisure so much as to eat. And they went 32 away in the boat to a desert place apart. And the people 33 saw them going, and many knew them, and they ran there together on foot from all the cities, and outwent them. And he came forth and saw a great multitude, and 34 he had compassion on them, because they were as sheep not having a shepherd: and he began to teach them many things. And when the day was now far spent, his disciples 35 came unto him, and said, The place is desert, and the day is now far spent: send them away, that they may go into 36 the country and villages round about, and buy themselves somewhat to eat. But he answered and said unto them, 37 Give ye them to eat. And they say unto him, Shall we go and buy two hundred pennyworth of bread, and give them to eat? And he saith unto them, How many loaves 38 have ye? go and see. And when they knew, they say, Five, and two fishes. And he commanded them that all 39 should sit down by companies upon the green grass. And 40 they sat down in ranks, by hundreds, and by fifties. And 41 he took the five loaves and the two fishes, and looking up to heaven, he blessed, and brake the loaves; and he gave to the disciples to set before them; and the two fishes divided he among them all. And they did all eat, and 42 were filled. And they took up broken pieces, twelve 43 basketfuls, and also of the fishes. And they that ate the 44 loaves were five thousand men.

¹And straightway he constrained his disciples to enter 45 into the boat, and to go before him unto the other side to

---

¹ The sections from this verse to viii. 26 are not found in Lk.

Bethsaida,[1] while he himself sendeth the multitude away.
46 And after he had taken leave of them, he departed into
47 the mountain to pray. And when even was come, the
boat was in the midst of the sea, and he alone on the land.
48 And seeing them distressed in rowing, for the wind was
contrary unto them, about the fourth watch of the night
he cometh unto them, walking on the sea; and he would
49 have passed by them: but they, when they saw him
walking on the sea, supposed that it was an apparition,
50 and cried out: for they all saw him, and were troubled.
But he straightway spake with them, and saith unto them,
51 Be of good cheer: it is I; be not afraid. And he went up
unto them into the boat; and the wind ceased: and they
52 were sore amazed in themselves; for they understood not
concerning the loaves, but their heart was hardened.

53   And when they had crossed over, they came to the land
54 unto Gennesaret, and moored to the shore. And when
they were come out of the boat, straightway the people
55 knew him, and ran round about that whole region, and
began to carry about on their beds those that were sick,
56 where they heard he was. And wheresoever he entered,
into villages, or into cities, or into the country, they laid
the sick in the marketplaces, and besought him that they
might touch if it were but the border of his garment: and
as many as touched him were made whole.

[1] At the north-east end of the lake and outside Galilee.

D. By Contrast with Tradition
(cf. pp. 64–6)

1. RENEWAL OF CONFLICT. DENUNCIATION OF THE RITUAL LAWS

7 And there are gathered together unto him the Pharisees, 1
and certain of the scribes, which had come from Jerusalem, and had seen that some of his disciples ate their 2
bread with defiled, that is, unwashen, hands. For the 3
Pharisees, and all the Jews, except they wash their hands
diligently,[1] eat not, holding the tradition of the elders:[2]
and when they come from the marketplace, except they 4
wash themselves, they eat not: and many other things
there be, which they have received to hold, washings of
cups, and pots, and brasen vessels. And the Pharisees 5
and the scribes ask him, Why walk not thy disciples
according to the tradition of the elders, but eat their
bread with defiled hands? And he said unto them, Well 6
did Isaiah prophesy of you hypocrites, as it is written,

This people honoureth me with their lips,
But their heart is far from me.
But in vain do they worship me, 7
Teaching as their doctrines the precepts of men.

Ye leave the commandment of God, and hold fast the 8
tradition of men. And he said unto them, Full well do 9
ye reject the commandment of God, that ye may keep
your tradition. For Moses said, Honour thy father and 10
thy mother; and, He that speaketh evil of father or
mother, let him die the death: but ye say, If a man shall 11

---

[1] Cf. for reading p. 37.   [2] Cf. p. 14.

say to his father or his mother, That wherewith thou
mightest have been profited by me is Corban, that is to
12 say, Given to God; ye no longer suffer him to do aught
13 for his father or his mother; making void the word of
God by your tradition, which ye have delivered: and
14 many such like things ye do. And he called to him the
multitude again, and said unto them, Hear me all of you,
15 and understand: there is nothing from without the man,
that going into him can defile him: but the things which
17 proceed out of the man are those that defile the man. And
when he was entered into the house from the multitude,
18 his disciples asked of him the parable. And he saith unto
them, Are ye so without understanding also? Perceive
ye not, that whatsoever from without goeth into the man,
19 it cannot defile him; because it goeth not into his heart,
but into his belly, and goeth out into the draught? This
20 he said, making all meats clean.[1] And he said, That
which proceedeth out of the man, that defileth the man.
21 For from within, out of the heart of men, evil thoughts
22 proceed, fornications, thefts, murders, adulteries, covet-
ings, wickednesses, deceit, lasciviousness, an evil eye,[2]
23 railing, pride, foolishness: all these evil things proceed
from within, and defile the man.

2. THE LONG JOURNEY: HEALING OF GENTILES

24   And from thence he arose, and went away into the
borders of Tyre and Sidon. And he entered into a house,
and would have no man know it: and he could not be hid.

---

[1] A note added by the Evangelist.
[2] I.e. envy: cf. Q, p. 176; Lk. xi. 34; Mt. vi. 23.

But straightway a woman, whose little daughter had an 25
unclean spirit, having heard of him, came and fell down
at his feet. Now the woman was a Greek,[1] a Syro- 26
phœnician by race. And she besought him that he would
cast forth the devil out of her daughter. And he said unto 27
her, Let the children first be filled: for it is not meet to
take the children's bread and cast it to the dogs. But she 28
answered and saith unto him, Yea, Lord: even the dogs
under the table eat of the children's crumbs. And he said 29
unto her, For this saying go thy way; the devil is gone out
of thy daughter. And she went away unto her house, and 30
found the child laid upon the bed, and the devil gone out.

And again he went out from the borders of Tyre, and 31
came through Sidon unto the sea of Galilee, through the
midst of the borders of Decapolis. And they bring unto 32
him one that was deaf, and had an impediment in his
speech; and they beseech him to lay his hand upon him.
And he took him aside from the multitude privately, and 33
put his fingers into his ears, and he spat, and touched his
tongue; and looking up to heaven, he sighed, and saith 34
unto him, Ephphatha, that is, Be opened. And his ears 35
were opened, and the bond of his tongue was loosed, and
he spake plain. And he charged them that they should 36
tell no man: but the more he charged them, so much the
more a great deal they published it. And they were 37
beyond measure astonished, saying, He hath done all
8 things well: he maketh even the deaf to hear, and the
dumb to speak.

In those days, when there was again a great multitude, 1
and they had nothing to eat, he called unto him his

---

[1] I.e. a Greek-speaking Gentile.

2 disciples, and saith unto them, I have compassion on the multitude, because they continue with me now three
3 days, and have nothing to eat: and if I send them away fasting to their home, they will faint in the way; and
4 some of them are come from far. And his disciples answered him, Whence shall one be able to fill these men
5 with bread here in a desert place? And he asked them,
6 How many loaves have ye? And they said, Seven. And he commandeth the multitude to sit down on the ground: and he took the seven loaves, and having given thanks, he brake, and gave to his disciples, to set before them; and
7 they set them before the multitude. And they had a few small fishes: and having blessed them, he commanded to
8 set these also before them. And they did eat, and were filled: and they took up, of broken pieces that remained
9 over, seven baskets.[1] And they were about four thousand:
10 and he sent them away. And straightway he entered into the boat with his disciples, and came into the parts of Dalmanutha.[2]

3. FINAL CONFLICT IN GALILEE

11 And the Pharisees came forth, and began to question with him, seeking of him a sign from heaven, tempting
12 him. And he sighed deeply in his spirit, and saith, Why doth this generation seek a sign? verily I say unto you,
13 There shall no sign be given unto this generation. And he left them, and again entering into the boat departed to the other side.

[1] A different basket from that in vi. 43: this is much larger; cf. Acts ix. 25.
[2] Cf. p. 38.

And they forgot to take bread; and they had not in the 14
boat with them more than one loaf. And he charged 15
them, saying, Take heed, beware of the leaven of the
Pharisees and the leaven of Herod. And they reasoned 16
one with another, saying, We have no bread. And Jesus 17
perceiving it saith unto them, Why reason ye, because
ye have no bread? do ye not yet perceive, neither understand? have ye your heart hardened? Having eyes, see 18
ye not? and having ears, hear ye not? and do ye not
remember? When I brake the five loaves among the five 19
thousand, how many baskets full of broken pieces took
ye up? They say unto him, Twelve. And when the seven 20
among the four thousand, how many basketfuls of
broken pieces took ye up? And they say unto him, Seven.
And he said unto them, Do ye not yet understand? 21

And they come unto Bethsaida. And they bring to him 22
a blind man, and beseech him to touch him. And he took 23
hold of the blind man by the hand, and brought him out
of the village; and when he had spit on his eyes, and laid
his hands upon him, he asked him, Seest thou aught?
And he looked up, and said, I see men; for I behold them 24
as trees, walking. Then again he laid his hands upon his 25
eyes; and he looked stedfastly, and was restored, and saw
all things clearly. And he sent him away to his home, 26
saying, Do not even enter into the village.

E. BY CHALLENGE AND REVELATION
(cf. pp. 66–8)

1. THE CONFESSION OF PETER

27 And Jesus went forth, and his disciples, into the villages of Cæsarea Philippi: and in the way he asked his disciples, saying unto them, Who do men say that I am?
28 And they told him, saying, John the Baptist: and others,
29 Elijah; but others, One of the prophets. And he asked them, But who say ye that I am? Peter answereth and
30 saith unto him, Thou art the Christ.[1] And he charged
31 them that they should tell no man of him. And he began to teach them, that the Son of man must suffer many things, and be rejected by the elders, and the chief priests, and the scribes, and be killed, and after three days rise
32 again. And he spake the saying openly. And Peter took
33 him, and began to rebuke him. But he turning about, and seeing his disciples, rebuked Peter, and saith, Get thee behind me, Satan: for thou mindest not the things
34 of God, but the things of men. And he called unto him the multitude with his disciples, and said unto them, If any man would come after me, let him deny himself, and
35 take up his cross, and follow me. For whosoever would save his life shall lose it; and whosoever shall lose his life
36 for my sake and the gospel's shall save it.[2] For what doth it profit a man, to gain the whole world, and forfeit his
37 life? For what should a man give in exchange for his life?
38 For whosoever shall be ashamed of me and of my words in this adulterous and sinful generation, the Son of man

[1] I.e. the Messiah; cf. p. 26.
[2] Cf. Q, p. 186; Lk. xvii. 33; Mt. x. 39; Jn. xii. 25.

also shall be ashamed of him, when he cometh in the glory of his Father with the holy angels.

9 And he said unto them, Verily I say unto you, There be 1 some here of them that stand by, which shall in no wise taste of death, till they see the kingdom of God come with power.

2. THE TRANSFIGURATION

And after six days Jesus taketh with him Peter, and 2 James, and John, and bringeth them up into a high mountain apart by themselves: and he was transfigured before them: and his garments became glistering, ex- 3 ceeding white; so as no fuller on earth can whiten them. And there appeared unto them Elijah with Moses: and 4 they were talking with Jesus. And Peter answereth and 5 saith to Jesus, Rabbi, it is good for us to be here: and let us make three tabernacles; one for thee, and one for Moses, and one for Elijah. For he wist not what to 6 answer; for they became sore afraid. And there came a 7 cloud overshadowing them: and there came a voice out of the cloud, This is my beloved Son: hear ye him.[1] And 8 suddenly looking round about, they saw no one any more, save Jesus only with themselves.

And as they were coming down from the mountain, 9 he charged them that they should tell no man what things they had seen, save when the Son of man should have risen again from the dead. And they kept the saying, 10 questioning among themselves what the rising again from the dead should mean. And they asked him, saying, The 11

---

[1] Cf. Mk. i. 11.

12 scribes say that Elijah must first come. And he said unto them, Elijah indeed cometh first, and restoreth all things: and how is it written of the Son of man, that he should
13 suffer many things and be set at nought? But I say unto you, that Elijah is come,[1] and they have also done unto him whatsoever they listed, even as it is written of him.[2]

3. THE HEALING OF THE EPILEPTIC

14   And when they came to the disciples, they saw a great multitude about them, and scribes questioning with
15 them. And straightway all the multitude, when they saw him, were greatly amazed, and running to him saluted
16 him. And he asked them, What question ye with them?
17 And one of the multitude answered him, Master, I brought unto thee my son, which hath a dumb spirit;
18 and wheresoever it taketh him, it dasheth him down: and he foameth, and grindeth his teeth, and pineth away: and I spake to thy disciples that they should cast it out;
19 and they were not able. And he answereth them and saith, O faithless generation, how long shall I be with you? how long shall I bear with you? bring him unto me.
20 And they brought him unto him: and when he saw him, straightway the spirit tare him grievously; and he fell on
21 the ground, and wallowed foaming. And he asked his father, How long time is it since this hath come unto
22 him? And he said, From a child. And oft-times it hath cast him both into the fire and into the waters, to destroy

---

[1] Mt. xvii. 13 adds that the disciples understood that Elijah symbolised John the Baptist.
[2] I.e. Herodias had done to John what Jezebel had threatened to do to Elijah.

him: but if thou canst do anything, have compassion on us, and help us. And Jesus said unto him, If thou canst! 23 All things are possible to him that believeth. Straightway 24 the father of the child cried out, and said, I believe; help thou mine unbelief. And when Jesus saw that a multitude 25 came running together, he rebuked the unclean spirit, saying unto him, Thou dumb and deaf spirit, I command thee, come out of him, and enter no more into him. And 26 having cried out, and torn him much, he came out: and the child became as one dead; insomuch that the more part said, He is dead. But Jesus took him by the hand, 27 and raised him up; and he arose. And when he was come 28 into the house, his disciples asked him privately, saying, We could not cast it out. And he said unto them, This 29 kind can come out by nothing, save by prayer.

III. THE CRISIS

A. THE JOURNEY TO JERUSALEM—THE CONSEQUENCES OF THEIR CONFESSION
(cf. pp. 68–71)

1. THE CHARACTER OF MESSIAHSHIP: SECRETLY THROUGH GALILEE

And they went forth from thence, and passed through 30 Galilee; and he would not that any man should know it. For he taught his disciples, and said unto them, The 31 Son of man is delivered up into the hands of men, and they shall kill him; and when he is killed, after three days

32 he shall rise again. But they understood not the saying, and were afraid to ask him.

33 And they came to Capernaum: and when he was in the house he asked them, What were ye reasoning in the way?

34 But they held their peace: for they had disputed one with

35 another in the way, who was the greatest. And he sat down, and called the twelve; and he saith unto them, If any man would be first, he shall be last of all, and

36 minister of all. And he took a little child, and set him in the midst of them: and taking him in his arms, he said

37 unto them, Whosoever shall receive one of such little children in my name,[1] receiveth me: and whosoever receiveth me, receiveth not me, but him that sent me.

38 John said unto him, Master, we saw one casting out devils in thy name: and we forbade him, because he

39 followed not us. But Jesus said, Forbid him not: for there is no man which shall do a mighty work in my name,

40 and be able quickly to speak evil of me. For he that is not

41 against us is for us.[2] For whosoever shall give you a cup of water to drink, because ye are Christ's, verily I say

42 unto you, he shall in no wise lose his reward. And whosoever shall cause one of these little ones that believe on me to stumble, it were better for him if a great mill-stone were hanged about his neck, and he were cast into

43 the sea. And if thy hand cause thee to stumble, cut it off: it is good for thee to enter into life maimed, rather than having thy two hands to go into hell, into the un-

45 quenchable fire. And if thy foot cause thee to stumble,

[1] I.e. for my sake.

[2] Cf. Q, p. 175; Lk. xi. 23; Mt. xii. 30. Here the saying deals with conduct and a spirit of tolerance; there with personal relationship to Christ and the need for decision.

cut it off: it is good for thee to enter into life halt, rather than having thy two feet to be cast into hell. And if thine 47 eye cause thee to stumble, cast it out: it is good for thee to enter into the kingdom of God with one eye, rather than having two eyes to be cast into hell; where their 48 worm dieth not, and the fire is not quenched.[1] For every 49 one shall be salted with fire. Salt is good: but if the salt 50 have lost its saltness, wherewith will ye season it? Have salt in yourselves, and be at peace one with another.

2. CONDITIONS OF DISCIPLESHIP: PUBLIC MINISTRY IN JUDÆA
(cf. pp. 69–71)

0 And he arose from thence, and cometh into the borders 1 of Judæa and beyond Jordan: and multitudes come together unto him again; and, as he was wont, he taught them again. And there came unto him Pharisees, and 2 asked him, Is it lawful for a man to put away his wife? tempting him. And he answered and said unto them, 3 What did Moses command you? And they said, Moses 4 suffered to write a bill of divorcement, and to put her away.[2] But Jesus said unto them, For your hardness of 5 heart he wrote you this commandment. But from the 6 beginning of the creation, Male and female made he them.[3] For this cause shall a man leave his father and 7 mother, and shall cleave to his wife; and the twain shall 8 become one flesh: so that they are no more twain, but one flesh.[4] What therefore God hath joined together, let not 9

[1] From Isaiah lxvi. 25 describing the corruption in the valley of Hinnom.
[2] Cf. Deut. xxiv. 1.   [3] Gen. i. 27.   [4] Gen. ii. 24.

10 man put asunder. And in the house the disciples asked
11 him again of this matter. And he saith unto them,
Whosoever shall put away his wife, and marry another,
12 committeth adultery against her: and if she herself shall
put away her husband, and marry another, she committeth adultery.

13 And they brought unto him little children, that he
14 should touch them: and the disciples rebuked them. But
when Jesus saw it, he was moved with indignation, and
said unto them, Suffer the little children to come unto
me; forbid them not: for of such is the kingdom of God.
15 Verily I say unto you, Whosoever shall not receive the
kingdom of God as a little child, he shall in no wise enter
16 therein. And he took them in his arms, and blessed
them, laying his hands upon them.

17 And as he was going forth into the way, there ran one
to him, and kneeled to him, and asked him, Good Master,
18 what shall I do that I may inherit eternal life? And Jesus
said unto him, Why callest thou me good? none is good
19 save one, even God.[1] Thou knowest the commandments, Do not kill, Do not commit adultery, Do not steal,
Do not bear false witness, Do not defraud, Honour thy
20 father and mother. And he said unto him, Master, all
21 these things have I observed from my youth. And Jesus
looking upon him loved him, and said unto him, One
thing thou lackest: go, sell whatsoever thou hast, and
give to the poor, and thou shalt have treasure in heaven:
22 and come, follow me. But his countenance fell at the
saying, and he went away sorrowful: for he was one that
had great possessions.

[1] Cf. p. 97.

And Jesus looked round about, and saith unto his 23
disciples, How hardly shall they that have riches enter
into the kingdom of God! And the disciples were 24
amazed at his words. But Jesus answereth again, and
saith unto them, Children, how hard is it for them that
trust in riches to enter into the kingdom of God! It is 25
easier for a camel to go through a needle's eye, than for
a rich man to enter into the kingdom of God. And they 26
were astonished exceedingly, saying unto him, Then
who can be saved? Jesus looking upon them saith, With 27
men it is impossible, but not with God: for all things are
possible with God. Peter began to say unto him, Lo, we 28
have left all, and have followed thee. Jesus said, Verily 29
I say unto you, There is no man that hath left house, or
brethren, or sisters, or mother, or father, or children, or
lands, for my sake, and for the gospel's sake, but he shall 30
receive a hundredfold now in this time, houses, and
brethren, and sisters, and mothers, and children, and
lands, with persecutions; and in the world to come eternal
life. But many that are first shall be last; and the last 31
first.

3. THE COST OF DISCIPLESHIP: THE ROAD TO JERICHO

And they were in the way, going up to Jerusalem; and 32
Jesus was going before them: and they were amazed;
and they that followed were afraid. And he took again
the twelve, and began to tell them the things that were to
happen unto him, saying, Behold, we go up to Jeru- 33
salem; and the Son of man shall be delivered unto the
chief priests and the scribes; and they shall condemn him

34 to death, and shall deliver him unto the Gentiles: and they shall mock him, and shall spit upon him, and shall scourge him, and shall kill him; and after three days he shall rise again.

35 And there come near unto him James and John, the sons of Zebedee, saying unto him, Master, we would that thou shouldest do for us whatsoever we shall ask of thee.
36 And he said unto them, What would ye that I should do
37 for you? And they said unto him, Grant unto us that we may sit, one on thy right hand, and one on thy left hand,
38 in thy glory. But Jesus said unto them, Ye know not what ye ask. Are ye able to drink the cup that I drink?[1] or to be baptized with the baptism that I am baptized
39 with?[2] And they said unto him, We are able. And Jesus said unto them, The cup that I drink ye shall drink; and with the baptism that I am baptized withal shall ye be
40 baptized: but to sit on my right hand or on my left hand is not mine to give: but it is for them for whom it hath
41 been prepared. And when the ten heard it, they began to be moved with indignation concerning James and
42 John. And Jesus called them to him, and saith unto them, Ye know that they which are accounted to rule over the Gentiles lord it over them; and their great ones
43 exercise authority over them. But it is not so among you: but whosoever would become great among you,
44 shall be your minister: and whosoever would be first
45 among you, shall be servant of all. For verily the Son of man came not to be ministered unto, but to minister, and to give his life a ransom for many.

46 And they come to Jericho: and as he went out from

---

[1] Cf. Mk. xiv. 36.   [2] Cf. Lk. xii. 50.

Jericho, with his disciples and a great multitude, the son
of Timæus, Bartimæus, a blind beggar, was sitting by
the way side. And when he heard that it was Jesus of 47
Nazareth, he began to cry out, and say, Jesus, thou son
of David, have mercy on me. And many rebuked him, 48
that he should hold his peace: but he cried out the more
a great deal, Thou son of David, have mercy on me. And 49
Jesus stood still, and said, Call ye him. And they call the
blind man, saying unto him, Be of good cheer: rise, he
calleth thee. And he, casting away his garment, sprang 50
up, and came to Jesus. And Jesus answered him, and 51
said, What wilt thou that I should do unto thee? And
the blind man said unto him, Rabboni, that I may receive
my sight. And Jesus said unto him, Go thy way; thy 52
faith hath made thee whole. And straightway he received
his sight, and followed him in the way.

B. The Claim to Messiahship

(cf. pp. 71–5)

1. IN ACTION

1 And when they draw nigh unto Jerusalem, unto Beth- 1
phage and Bethany, at the mount of Olives, he sendeth
two of his disciples, and saith unto them, Go your way 2
into the village that is over against you: and straightway
as ye enter into it, ye shall find a colt tied, whereon no
man ever yet sat; loose him, and bring him. And if any 3
one say unto you, Why do ye this? say ye, The Lord hath
need of him; and straightway he will send him back
hither. And they went away, and found a colt tied at the 4

5 door without in the open street; and they loose him. And certain of them that stood there said unto them, What do
6 ye, loosing the colt? And they said unto them even as
7 Jesus had said: and they let them go. And they bring the colt unto Jesus, and cast on him their garments; and he
8 sat upon him. And many spread their garments upon the way; and others branches, which they had cut from the
9 fields. And they that went before, and they that followed, cried, Hosanna;[1] Blessed is he that cometh in the name
10 of the Lord: Blessed is the kingdom that cometh, the kingdom of our father David: Hosanna in the highest.

11   And he entered into Jerusalem, into the temple; and when he had looked round about upon all things, it being now eventide, he went out unto Bethany with the twelve.

12   And on the morrow, when they were come out from
13 Bethany, he hungered. And seeing a fig tree afar off having leaves, he came, if haply he might find anything thereon: and when he came to it, he found nothing but
14 leaves; for it was not the season of figs. And he answered and said unto it, No man eat fruit from thee henceforward for ever. And his disciples heard it.

15   And they come to Jerusalem: and he entered into the temple, and began to cast out them that sold and them that bought in the temple, and overthrew the tables of the money-changers, and the seats of them that sold the
16 doves; and he would not suffer that any man should carry
17 a vessel through the temple. And he taught, and said unto them, Is it not written, My house shall be called a house of prayer for all the nations? but ye have made it
18 a den of robbers. And the chief priests and the scribes

[1] I.e. Save now; cf. Ps. cxviii. 25.

heard it,[1] and sought how they might destroy him: for they feared him, for all the multitude was astonished at his teaching.

And every evening he went forth out of the city.   19

And as they passed by in the morning, they saw the fig 20
tree withered away from the roots. And Peter calling to 21
remembrance saith unto him, Rabbi, behold, the fig tree which thou cursedst is withered away. And Jesus an- 22
swering saith unto them, Have faith in God. Verily I say 23
unto you, Whosoever shall say unto this mountain, Be thou taken up and cast into the sea; and shall not doubt in his heart, but shall believe that what he saith cometh to pass; he shall have it. Therefore I say unto you, All 24
things whatsoever ye pray and ask for, believe that ye have received them, and ye shall have them. And when- 25
soever ye stand praying, forgive, if ye have aught against any one; that your Father also which is in heaven may forgive you your trespasses.

2. IN TEACHING

And they come again to Jerusalem: and as he was 27
walking in the temple, there come to him the chief priests, and the scribes, and the elders; and they said unto him, 28
By what authority doest thou these things? or who gave thee this authority to do these things? And Jesus said 29
unto them, I will ask of you one question, and answer me, and I will tell you by what authority I do these things. The baptism of John, was it from heaven, or from men? 30
answer me. And they reasoned with themselves, saying, 31

[1] Cf. p. 19.

If we shall say, From heaven; he will say, Why then did
32 ye not believe him? But should we say, From men—
they feared the people: for all verily held John to be a
33 prophet. And they answered Jesus and say, We know
not. And Jesus saith unto them, Neither tell I you by
what authority I do these things.

12 1 And he began to speak unto them in parables. A man
planted a vineyard, and set a hedge about it, and digged
a pit for the winepress, and built a tower, and let it out
2 to husbandmen, and went into another country. And at
the season he sent to the husbandmen a servant, that he
might receive from the husbandmen of the fruits of the
3 vineyard. And they took him, and beat him, and sent
4 him away empty. And again he sent unto them another
servant; and him they wounded in the head, and handled
5 shamefully. And he sent another; and him they killed:
6 and many others; beating some, and killing some. He
had yet one, a beloved son: he sent him last unto them,
7 saying, They will reverence my son. But those husbandmen said among themselves, This is the heir; come, let
8 us kill him, and the inheritance shall be ours. And they
took him, and killed him, and cast him forth out of the
9 vineyard. What therefore will the lord of the vineyard do?
he will come and destroy the husbandmen, and will give
10 the vineyard unto others. Have ye not read even this
scripture;[1]

　　　The stone which the builders rejected,
　　　The same was made the head of the corner:
11　　　This was from the Lord,
　　　And it is marvellous in our eyes?

　　　　　　[1] Ps. cxviii. 22–3; cf. Mk. xi. 9.

And they sought to lay hold on him; and they feared the 12
multitude; for they perceived that he spake the parable
against them: and they left him, and went away.

3. IN ANSWER TO QUESTIONS

And they send unto him certain of the Pharisees and 13
of the Herodians,[1] that they might catch him in talk.
And when they were come, they say unto him, Master, 14
we know that thou art true, and carest not for any one:
for thou regardest not the person of men, but of a truth
teachest the way of God: Is it lawful to give tribute unto
Cæsar, or not? Shall we give, or shall we not give? But 15
he, knowing their hypocrisy, said unto them, Why
tempt ye me? bring me a penny,[2] that I may see it. And 16
they brought it. And he saith unto them, Whose is this
image and superscription? And they said unto him,
Cæsar's. And Jesus said unto them, Render unto Cæsar 17
the things that are Cæsar's, and unto God the things that
are God's. And they marvelled greatly at him.

And there come unto him Sadducees, which say that 18
there is no resurrection;[3] and they asked him, saying,
Master, Moses[4] wrote unto us, If a man's brother die, 19
and leave a wife behind him, and leave no child, that his
brother should take his wife, and raise up seed unto his
brother. There were seven brethren: and the first took 20
a wife, and dying left no seed; and the second took her, 21
and died, leaving no seed behind him; and the third

[1] Cf. p. 18.
[2] I.e. a Roman denarius, which would have to be brought from
outside the Temple.   [3] Cf. p. 18.
[4] Deut. xxv. 5–10, the law of Levirate Marriage.

22 likewise: and the seven left no seed. Last of all the woman
23 also died. In the resurrection whose wife shall she be of
24 them? for the seven had her to wife. Jesus said unto them,
Is it not for this cause that ye err, that ye know not the
25 scriptures, nor the power of God? For when they shall
rise from the dead, they neither marry, nor are given in
26 marriage; but are as angels in heaven. But as touching
the dead, that they are raised; have ye not read in the
book of Moses, in the place concerning the Bush,[1] how
God spake unto him, saying, I am the God of Abraham,
27 and the God of Isaac, and the God of Jacob? He is not
the God of the dead, but of the living: ye do greatly err.
28 And one of the scribes came, and heard them questioning together, and knowing that he had answered
them well, asked him, What commandment is the first
29 of all? Jesus answered, The first is, Hear, O Israel; The
30 Lord our God, the Lord is one: and thou shalt love the
Lord thy God with all thy heart, and with all thy soul,
31 and with all thy mind, and with all thy strength.[2] The
second is this, Thou shalt love thy neighbour as thyself.[3]
There is none other commandment greater than these.
32 And the scribe said unto him, Of a truth, Master, thou
hast well said that he is one; and there is none other but
33 he: and to love him with all the heart, and with all the
understanding, and with all the strength, and to love his
neighbour as himself, is much more than all whole burnt
34 offerings and sacrifices. And when Jesus saw that he
answered discreetly, he said unto him, Thou art not far
from the kingdom of God. And no man after that durst
ask him any question.

[1] Exod. iii. 1 ff.   [2] Deut. vi. 4, 5.   [3] Levit. xix. 18.

And Jesus answered and said, as he taught in the 35
temple, How say the scribes that the Christ is the son of
David? David himself said in the Holy Spirit,   36
    The Lord said unto my Lord,
    Sit thou on my right hand,
    Till I make thine enemies the footstool of thy feet.[1]
David himself calleth him Lord; and whence is he his 37
son? And the common people heard him gladly.

4. BY WARNING

And in his teaching he said, Beware of the scribes, 38
which desire to walk in long robes, and to have salutations
in the marketplaces, and chief seats in the synagogues, 39
and chief places at feasts:[2] they which devour widows' 40
houses, and for a pretence make long prayers; these shall
receive greater condemnation.

And he sat down over against the treasury, and beheld 41
how the multitude cast money into the treasury: and
many that were rich cast in much. And there came a poor 42
widow, and she cast in two mites, which make a farthing.
And he called unto him his disciples, and said unto them, 43
Verily I say unto you, This poor widow cast in more than
all they which are casting into the treasury: for they all 44
did cast in of their superfluity; but she of her want did
cast in all that she had, even all her living.

3 And as he went forth out of the temple, one of his 1
disciples saith unto him, Master, behold, what manner of
stones and what manner of buildings! And Jesus said 2

---

[1] Ps. cx. 1: a psalm traditionally ascribed to David.
[2] Cf. Q, p. 177; Lk. xi. 43; Mt. xxiii. 6, 7.

unto him, Seest thou these great buildings? there shall not be left here one stone upon another, which shall not be thrown down.

[AN APOCALYPTIC DISCOURSE[1]; cf. pp. 99–100]

3 And as he sat on the mount of Olives over against the temple, Peter and James and John and Andrew asked 4 him privately, Tell us, when shall these things be? and what shall be the sign when these things are all about to 5 be accomplished? And Jesus began to say unto them, 6 Take heed that no man lead you astray. Many shall come in my name, saying, I am he; and shall lead many astray. 7 And when ye shall hear of wars and rumours of wars, be not troubled: these things must needs come to pass; but 8 the end is not yet. For nation shall rise against nation, and kingdom against kingdom: there shall be earthquakes in divers places; there shall be famines: these things are the beginning of travail.

9 But take ye heed to yourselves: for they shall deliver you up to councils; and in synagogues shall ye be beaten; and before governors and kings shall ye stand for my 10 sake, for a testimony unto them. And the gospel must 11 first be preached unto all the nations. And when they lead you to judgement, and deliver you up, be not anxious beforehand what ye shall speak: but whatsoever shall be given you in that hour, that speak ye: for it is not 12 ye that speak, but the Holy Ghost. And brother shall deliver up brother to death, and the father his child; and children shall rise up against parents, and cause them to

[1] This appears to be drawn from a written source incorporated in the Gospel by the Evangelist: cf. *v.* 14.

be put to death. And ye shall be hated of all men for my 13
name's sake: but he that endureth to the end, the same
shall be saved.

But when ye see the abomination of desolation 14
standing where he ought not[1] (let him that readeth
understand), then let them that are in Judæa flee unto
the mountains: and let him that is on the housetop not 15
go down, nor enter in, to take anything out of his house:
and let him that is in the field not return back to take his 16
cloke. But woe unto them that are with child and to them 17
that give suck in those days! And pray ye that it be not 18
in the winter. For those days shall be tribulation, such 19
as there hath not been the like from the beginning of the
creation which God created until now, and never shall
be. And except the Lord had shortened the days, no 20
flesh would have been saved: but for the elect's sake,
whom he chose, he shortened the days. And then if any 21
man shall say unto you, Lo, here is the Christ; or, Lo,
there; believe it not: for there shall arise false Christs and 22
false prophets, and shall shew signs and wonders, that
they may lead astray, if possible, the elect. But take ye 23
heed: behold, I have told you all things beforehand.

But in those days, after that tribulation, the sun shall 24
be darkened, and the moon shall not give her light, and 25
the stars shall be falling from heaven, and the powers
that are in the heavens shall be shaken. And then shall 26
they see the Son of man coming in clouds with great
power and glory.[2] And then shall he send forth the angels, 27

[1] Cf. Dan. ix. 27, etc., and 1 Macc. i. 54: a cryptic reference to
the altar of Zeus Olympios erected by Antiochus in the Temple.
Lk. xxi. 20 interprets it as "Jerusalem compassed with camps".

[2] Cf. Mk. xiv. 62.

and shall gather together his elect from the four winds, from the uttermost part of the earth to the uttermost part of heaven.

28 Now from the fig tree learn her parable: when her branch is now become tender, and putteth forth its
29 leaves, ye know that the summer is nigh; even so ye also, when ye see these things coming to pass, know ye that
30 he is nigh, even at the doors. Verily I say unto you, This generation shall not pass away, until all these things be
31 accomplished. Heaven and earth shall pass away: but
32 my words shall not pass away. But of that day or that hour knoweth no one, not even the angels in heaven,
33 neither the Son, but the Father. Take ye heed, watch and
34 pray: for ye know not when the time is. It is as when a man, sojourning in another country, having left his
35 house, and given authority to his servants, to each one his work, commanded also the porter to watch. Watch therefore: for ye know not when the lord of the house
36 cometh, whether at even, or at midnight, or at cock-
37 crowing, or in the morning; lest coming suddenly he find you sleeping. And what I say unto you I say unto all, Watch.

C. THE BETRAYAL
(cf. p. 75)

1. THE PREPARATION

14 1 Now after two days was the feast of the passover and the unleavened bread: and the chief priests and the scribes
. sought how they might take him with subtilty, and kill

him: for they said, Not during the feast, lest haply there 2
shall be a tumult of the people.

And while he was in Bethany[1] in the house of Simon 3
the leper, as he sat at meat, there came a woman having
an alabaster cruse of ointment of spikenard very costly;
and she brake the cruse, and poured it over his head.
But there were some that had indignation among them- 4
selves, saying, To what purpose hath this waste of the
ointment been made? For this ointment might have 5
been sold for above three hundred pence,[2] and given to
the poor. And they murmured against her. But Jesus 6
said, Let her alone; why trouble ye her? she hath wrought
a good work on me. For ye have the poor always with 7
you, and whensoever ye will ye can do them good: but
me ye have not always. She hath done what she could: 8
she hath anointed my body aforehand for the burying.
And verily I say unto you, Wheresoever the gospel shall 9
be preached throughout the whole world, that also which
this woman hath done shall be spoken of for a memorial
of her.

And Judas Iscariot, he that was one of the twelve, 10
went away unto the chief priests, that he might deliver
him unto them. And they, when they heard it, were 11
glad, and promised to give him money. And he sought
how he might conveniently deliver him unto them.

[1] Cf. Jn. xii. 2–8.
[2] I.e. denarii; cf. xii. 15.

2. THE LAST SUPPER

12 And on the first day of unleavened bread, when they sacrificed the passover,[1] his disciples say unto him, Where wilt thou that we go and make ready that thou
13 mayest eat the passover? And he sendeth two of his disciples, and saith unto them, Go into the city, and there shall meet you a man bearing a pitcher of water:
14 follow him; and wheresoever he shall enter in, say to the goodman of the house, The Master saith, Where is my guest-chamber, where I shall eat the passover with my
15 disciples? And he will himself shew you a large upper room furnished and ready: and there make ready for us.
16 And the disciples went forth, and came into the city, and found as he had said unto them: and they made ready the passover.

17 And when it was evening he cometh with the twelve.
18 And as they sat and were eating, Jesus said, Verily I say unto you, One of you shall betray me, even he that eateth
19 with me. They began to be sorrowful, and to say unto
20 him one by one, Is it I? And he said unto them, It is one
21 of the twelve, he that dippeth with me in the dish. For the Son of man goeth, even as it is written of him: but woe unto that man through whom the Son of man is betrayed! good were it for that man if he had not been born.

22 And as they were eating,[2] he took bread, and when he had blessed, he brake it, and gave to them, and said, Take

---

[1] Jn. xiii. 29, etc., dates the Supper one day earlier; and this date is probably correct.

[2] For other accounts cf. Mt. xxvi. 26–9; Lk. xxii. 17–20; 1 Cor. xi. 23–5; and p. 101.

ye : this is my body. And he took a cup, and when he had 23
given thanks, he gave to them: and they all drank of it.
And he said unto them, This is my blood of the covenant, 24
which is shed for many. Verily I say unto you, I will no 25
more drink of the fruit of the vine, until that day when
I drink it new in the kingdom of God.

3. THE AGONY IN THE GARDEN

And when they had sung a hymn,[1] they went out unto 26
the mount of Olives.

And Jesus saith unto them, All ye shall be offended: 27
for it is written, I will smite the shepherd, and the sheep
shall be scattered abroad. Howbeit, after I am raised up, 28
I will go before you into Galilee. But Peter said unto 29
him, Although all shall be offended, yet will not I. And 30
Jesus saith unto him, Verily I say unto thee, that thou
to-day, even this night, before the cock crow twice, shalt
deny me thrice. But he spake exceeding vehemently, 31
If I must die with thee, I will not deny thee. And in like
manner also said they all.

And they come unto a place which was named 32
Gethsemane: and he saith unto his disciples, Sit ye here,
while I pray. And he taketh with him Peter and James 33
and John, and began to be greatly amazed, and sore
troubled. And he saith unto them, My soul is exceeding 34
sorrowful even unto death: abide ye here, and watch.
And he went forward a little, and fell on the ground, and 35
prayed that, if it were possible, the hour might pass away
from him. And he said, Abba, Father, all things are 36

---

[1] Probably the Hallel (Pss. cxv–cxviii) usually sung at the Passover.

possible unto thee; remove this cup from me: howbeit
37 not what I will, but what thou wilt. And he cometh, and
findeth them sleeping, and saith unto Peter, Simon,
sleepest thou? couldest thou not watch one hour?
38 Watch and pray, that ye enter not into temptation: the
39 spirit indeed is willing, but the flesh is weak. And again
40 he went away, and prayed, saying the same words. And
again he came, and found them sleeping, for their eyes
were very heavy; and they wist not what to answer him.
41 And he cometh the third time, and saith unto them,
Sleep on now, and take your rest: it is enough; the hour
is come; behold, the Son of man is betrayed into the
42 hands of sinners. Arise, let us be going: behold, he that
betrayeth me is at hand.

43   And straightway, while he yet spake, cometh Judas,
one of the twelve, and with him a multitude with swords
and staves, from the chief priests and the scribes and the
44 elders. Now he that betrayed him had given them a
token, saying, Whomsoever I shall kiss, that is he; take
45 him, and lead him away safely. And when he was come,
straightway he came to him, and saith, Rabbi; and kissed
46, 47 him. And they laid hands on him, and took him. But
a certain one of them that stood by drew his sword, and
smote the servant of the high priest, and struck off his
48 ear.[1] And Jesus answered and said unto them, Are ye
come out, as against a robber, with swords and staves to
49 seize me? I was daily with you in the temple teaching,
and ye took me not: but this is done that the scriptures
50 might be fulfilled. And they all left him, and fled.

51   And a certain young man followed with him, having

[1] Jn. xviii. 10 adds the names of St Peter and Malchus.

a linen cloth cast about him, over his naked body: and
they lay hold on him; but he left the linen cloth, and fled 52
naked.[1]

D. THE TRIAL
(cf. p. 76)

1. BEFORE THE HIGH PRIEST

And they led Jesus away to the high priest: and there 53
come together with him all the chief priests and the elders
and the scribes. And Peter had followed him afar off, 54
even within, into the court of the high priest; and he was
sitting with the officers, and warming himself in the light
of the fire. Now the chief priests and the whole council 55
sought witness against Jesus to put him to death; and
found it not. For many bare false witness against him, 56
and their witness agreed not together. And there stood 57
up certain, and bare false witness against him, saying,
We heard him say, I will destroy this temple that is made 58
with hands, and in three days I will build another made
without hands.[2] And not even so did their witness agree 59
together. And the high priest stood up in the midst, and 60
asked Jesus, saying, Answerest thou nothing? what is it
which these witness against thee? But he held his peace, 61
and answered nothing. Again the high priest asked him,
and saith unto him, Art thou the Christ, the Son of the
Blessed? And Jesus said, I am: and ye shall see the Son 62
of man sitting at the right hand of power, and coming

[1] This incident is only recorded by St Mark, and may probably
be a personal reminiscence; cf. p. 40.
[2] Cf. Jn. ii. 19.

63 with the clouds of heaven.[1] And the high priest rent his clothes, and saith, What further need have we of wit-
64 nesses? Ye have heard the blasphemy:[2] what think ye?
65 And they all condemned him to be worthy of death. And some began to spit on him, and to cover his face, and to buffet him, and to say unto him, Prophesy: and the officers received him with blows of their hands.

66 And as Peter was beneath in the court, there cometh
67 one of the maids of the high priest; and seeing Peter warming himself, she looked upon him, and saith, Thou
68 also wast with the Nazarene, even Jesus. But he denied, saying, I neither know, nor understand what thou sayest:
69 and he went out into the porch; and the cock crew. And the maid saw him, and began again to say to them that
70 stood by, This is one of them. But he again denied it. And after a little while again they that stood by said to Peter, Of a truth thou art one of them; for thou art a
71 Galilæan. But he began to curse, and to swear, I know
72 not this man of whom ye speak. And straightway the second time the cock crew. And Peter called to mind the word, how that Jesus said unto him, Before the cock crow twice, thou shalt deny me thrice. And when he thought thereon, he wept.

2. BEFORE PILATE

15 1 And straightway in the morning the chief priests with the elders and scribes, and the whole council,[3] held a consultation, and bound Jesus, and carried him away,

---

[1] From Ps. cx. 1 and Dan. vii. 13.
[2] Cf. Mk. ii. 7, etc.: it is doubtful whether the claim to be Messiah was legally blasphemous.
[3] I.e. the Sanhedrin; cf. p. 22.

and delivered him up to Pilate.[1] And Pilate asked him, 2
Art thou the King of the Jews? And he answering saith
unto him, Thou sayest. And the chief priests accused 3
him of many things. And Pilate again asked him, saying, 4
Answerest thou nothing? behold how many things they
accuse thee of. But Jesus no more answered anything; 5
insomuch that Pilate marvelled.

Now at the feast he used to release unto them one 6
prisoner, whom they asked of him. And there was one 7
called Barabbas, lying bound with them that had made
insurrection, men who in the insurrection had committed
murder. And the multitude went up and began to ask 8
him to do as he was wont to do unto them. And Pilate 9
answered them, saying, Will ye that I release unto you
the King of the Jews? For he perceived that for envy 10
the chief priests had delivered him up. But the chief 11
priests stirred up the multitude, that he should rather
release Barabbas unto them. And Pilate again answered 12
and said unto them, What then shall I do unto him whom
ye call the King of the Jews? And they cried out again, 13
Crucify him. And Pilate said unto them, Why, what evil 14
hath he done? But they cried out exceedingly, Crucify
him. And Pilate, wishing to content the multitude, 15
released unto them Barabbas, and delivered Jesus, when
he had scourged him, to be crucified.

And the soldiers led him away within the court, which 16
is the Prætorium;[2] and they call together the whole band.
And they clothe him with purple, and plaiting a crown 17

[1] Cf. pp. 10, 11.
[2] Probably the Turris Antonia, the fort on the north-west of the
Temple.

18 of thorns, they put it on him; and they began to salute
19 him, Hail, King of the Jews! And they smote his head
with a reed, and did spit upon him, and bowing their
20 knees worshipped him. And when they had mocked him,
they took off from him the purple, and put on him his
garments. And they lead him out to crucify him.

E. THE CRUCIFIXION
(cf. pp. 76–7)

21   And they compel one passing by, Simon of Cyrene,
coming from the country, the father of Alexander and
Rufus,[1] to go with them, that he might bear his cross.
22 And they bring him unto the place Golgotha, which is,
23 being interpreted, The place of a skull. And they
offered him wine mingled with myrrh:[2] but he received
24 it not. And they crucify him, and part his garments
among them, casting lots upon them, what each should
25 take. And it was the third hour,[3] and they crucified him.
26 And the superscription of his accusation was written
27 over, THE KING OF THE JEWS. And with him they
crucify two robbers; one on his right hand, and one on
29 his left. And they that passed by railed on him, wagging
their heads, and saying, Ha! thou that destroyest the
30 temple, and buildest it in three days, save thyself, and
31 come down from the cross. In like manner also the chief
priests mocking him among themselves with the scribes

---

[1] These two must have been known to Mark and his readers;
cf. for Alexander Acts xix. 33 and Rufus Rom. xvi. 13.
[2] This was a narcotic to dull the pain.
[3] I.e. 9 a.m.

said, He saved others; himself he cannot save. Let the 32
Christ, the King of Israel, now come down from the
cross, that we may see and believe. And they that were
crucified with him reproached him.

And when the sixth hour was come, there was darkness 33
over the whole land until the ninth hour. And at the 34
ninth hour Jesus cried with a loud voice, Eloi, Eloi, lama
sabachthani? which is, being interpreted, My God, my
God, why hast thou forsaken me?[1] And some of them 35
that stood by, when they heard it, said, Behold, he calleth
Elijah. And one ran, and filling a sponge full of vinegar, 36
put it on a reed, and gave him to drink, saying, Let be;
let us see whether Elijah cometh to take him down. And 37
Jesus uttered a loud voice, and gave up the ghost. And 38
the veil of the temple was rent in twain from the top to
the bottom. And when the centurion, which stood by 39
over against him, saw that he so gave up the ghost, he
said, Truly this man was the Son of God. And there 40
were also women beholding from afar: among whom
were both Mary Magdalene,[2] and Mary the mother of
James the less and of Joses, and Salome;[3] who, when he 41
was in Galilee, followed him, and ministered unto him;
and many other women which came up with him unto
Jerusalem.

And when even was now come, because it was the 42
Preparation, that is, the day before the sabbath,[4] there 43
came Joseph of Arimathæa, a councillor of honourable
estate, who also himself was looking for the kingdom of

---

[1] From Ps. xxii. 1.   [2] Cf. Lk. viii. 2.
[3] Mt. xxvii. 56 calls her the mother of the sons of Zebedee.
[4] I.e. Friday.

God;[1] and he boldly went in unto Pilate, and asked for
44 the body of Jesus. And Pilate marvelled if he were
already dead: and calling unto him the centurion, he
45 asked him whether he had been any while dead. And
when he learned it of the centurion, he granted the corpse
46 to Joseph. And he bought a linen cloth, and taking him
down, wound him in the linen cloth, and laid him in a
tomb which had been hewn out of a rock; and he rolled
47 a stone against the door of the tomb. And Mary Magdalene and Mary the mother of Joses beheld where he
was laid.

F. THE RESURRECTION
(cf. pp. 77–8)

16 1 And when the sabbath was past, Mary Magdalene, and
Mary the mother of James, and Salome, bought spices,
2 that they might come and anoint him. And very early
on the first day of the week, they come to the tomb when
3 the sun was risen. And they were saying among themselves, Who shall roll us away the stone from the door of
4 the tomb? and looking up, they see that the stone is rolled
5 back: for it was exceeding great. And entering into the
tomb, they saw a young man sitting on the right side,
6 arrayed in a white robe; and they were amazed. And he
saith unto them, Be not amazed: ye seek Jesus, the
Nazarene, which hath been crucified: he is risen; he is
7 not here: behold, the place where they laid him! But
go, tell his disciples and Peter, He goeth before you into

---

[1] So Lk. ii. 25 of Simeon.

Galilee: there shall ye see him, as he said unto you.[1] And 8
they went out, and fled from the tomb; for trembling and
astonishment had come upon them: and they said nothing to any one; for they were afraid.[2]

[The following verses are not found in the oldest manuscripts
and differ wholly in style from the rest of the Gospel.]

Now when he was risen early on the first day of the 9
week, he appeared first to Mary Magdalene, from whom
he had cast out seven devils. She went and told them 10
that had been with him, as they mourned and wept. And 11
they, when they heard that he was alive, and had been
seen of her, disbelieved.

And after these things he was manifested in another 12
form unto two of them, as they walked, on their way into
the country. And they went away and told it unto the 13
rest: neither believed they them.

And afterward he was manifested unto the eleven 14
themselves as they sat at meat; and he upbraided them
with their unbelief and hardness of heart, because they
believed not them which had seen him after he was risen.
And he said unto them, Go ye into all the world, and 15
preach the gospel to the whole creation. He that be- 16
lieveth and is baptized shall be saved; but he that dis-
believeth shall be condemned. And these signs shall 17
follow them that believe: in my name shall they cast out
devils; they shall speak with new tongues; they shall take 18
up serpents, and if they drink any deadly thing, it shall in

[1] Cf. Mk. xiv. 28.   [2] Cf. p. 37.

no wise hurt them; they shall lay hands on the sick, and they shall recover.

19 So then the Lord Jesus, after he had spoken unto them, was received up into heaven, and sat down at the right
20 hand of God. And they went forth, and preached everywhere, the Lord working with them, and confirming the word by the signs that followed. Amen.

The Gospel contained in the source used in those according to St Matthew and St Luke—commonly known as "Q".

References in the left-hand margin give the origin of these passages in the Revised Version. On the right hand are references to the parallel account in the other Gospel.

I. THE GOOD NEWS

A. THE MESSAGE OF JOHN THE BAPTIST
(cf. Mk. i. 4–8 and p. 84)

Lk. iii. 7   John said therefore to the multitudes that went out to be baptized of him, Ye offspring of vipers, who warned you to flee from the 8 wrath to come? Bring forth therefore fruits worthy of repentance, and begin not to say within yourselves, We have Abraham to our father: for I say unto you, that God is able of these stones to raise up children unto 9 Abraham. And even now is the axe also laid unto the root of the trees: every tree therefore that bringeth not forth good fruit is hewn down, and cast into the fire.

16   [1] I indeed baptize you with water; but there cometh he that is mightier than I, the latchet of whose shoes I am not worthy to unloose:

= Mt. iii. 7–12

[1] Cf. Mk. i. 7–8.

he shall baptize you with the Holy Ghost and
17 with fire: whose fan is in his hand, throughly
to cleanse his threshing-floor, and to gather
the wheat into his garner; but the chaff he
will burn up with unquenchable fire.

B. THE TEMPTATION
(cf. Mk. i. 12, 13 and p. 53)

Lk. iv.

1 And Jesus was led by the Spirit in the
2 wilderness during forty days, being tempted
of the devil. And he did eat nothing in those
days: and when they were completed, he
3 hungered. And the devil said unto him, If
thou art the Son of God, command this stone
4 that it become bread. And Jesus answered
unto him, It is written, Man shall not live by
5 bread alone.[1] And he led him up, and shewed
him all the kingdoms of the world in a moment
6 of time. And the devil said unto him, To thee
will I give all these things, if thou wilt worship
8 me. And Jesus answered and said unto him,
It is written, Thou shalt worship the Lord
9 thy God, and him only shalt thou serve.[2] And
he led him to Jerusalem, and set him on the
pinnacle of the temple, and said unto him,
If thou art the Son of God, cast thyself down
10 from hence: for it is written,

He shall give his angels charge concerning
thee, to guard thee:

=Mt. iv.
11,but cha
ing the or
of second
third temp
tion.

[1] Deut. viii. 3.   [2] Deut. vi. 13.

11 and,

On their hands they shall bear thee up,
Lest haply thou dash thy foot against a
stone.[1]

12 And Jesus answering said unto him, It is said,
Thou shalt not tempt the Lord thy God.[2]

13 And the devil departed from him for a
season.

C. The Proclamation of the Kingdom
(cf. pp. 84–7)

k. vi. 20   And Jesus lifted up his eyes on his dis-   = Mt. v. 2–4,
ciples, and said, Blessed are ye poor: for yours   6, 11–12
21 is the kingdom of God. Blessed are ye that
hunger now: for ye shall be filled. Blessed are
22 ye that weep now: for ye shall laugh. Blessed
are ye, when men shall hate you, and when they
shall separate you from their company, and
reproach you, and cast out your name as evil,
23 for the Son of man's sake. Rejoice in that
day, and leap for joy: for behold, your reward
is great in heaven: for in the same manner did
24 their fathers unto the prophets. But woe unto
you that are rich! for ye have received your
25 consolation. Woe unto you, ye that are full
now! for ye shall hunger. Woe unto you, ye
that laugh now! for ye shall mourn and weep.

[1] Ps. xci. 11, 12.   [2] Deut. vi. 16.

26 Woe unto you, when all men shall speak well of you! for in the same manner did their fathers to the false prophets.

27 But I say unto you which hear, Love your
28 enemies, do good to them that hate you, bless them that curse you, pray for them that de-
29 spitefully use you. To him that smiteth thee on the one cheek offer also the other; and from him that taketh away thy cloke withhold not
30 thy coat also. Give to every one that asketh thee; and of him that taketh away thy goods
31 ask them not again. And as ye would that men should do to you, do ye also to them
32 likewise. And if ye love them that love you, what thank have ye? for even sinners love
33 those that love them. And if ye do good to them that do good to you, what thank have
34 ye? for even sinners do the same. And if ye lend to them of whom ye hope to receive, what thank have ye? even sinners lend to
35 sinners, to receive again as much. But love your enemies, and do them good, and lend, never despairing; and your reward shall be great, and ye shall be sons of the Most High: for he is kind toward the unthankful and evil.
36 Be ye merciful, even as your Father is merci-
37 ful. And judge not, and ye shall not be iudged: and condemn not, and ye shall not be condemned: release, and ye shall be
38 released: give, and it shall be given unto you; good measure, pressed down, shaken to-

= Mt. v. 4

= Mt. v. 39, 40, 42

= Mt. vii.

= Mt. v. 46-7

= Mt. vii. 1, 2

gether, running over, shall they give into your
bosom.[1] For with what measure ye mete it
shall be measured to you again.

39   Can the blind guide the blind? shall they   =Mt. xv. 14
40 not both fall into a pit? The disciple is not   =Mt. x. 24
above his master: but every one when he is
41 perfected shall be as his master. And why   =Mt. vii.
beholdest thou the mote[2] that is in thy brother's   3–5
eye, but considerest not the beam that is in
42 thine own eye? Or how canst thou say to thy
brother, Brother, let me cast out the mote that
is in thine eye, when thou thyself beholdest
not the beam that is in thine own eye? Thou
hypocrite, cast out first the beam out of thine
own eye, and then shalt thou see clearly to
cast out the mote that is in thy brother's eye.
43 For there is no good tree that bringeth forth   =Mt. vii. 16–
corrupt fruit; nor again a corrupt tree that   20 and xii.
44 bringeth forth good fruit. For each tree is   33–5
known by its own fruit. For of thorns men
do not gather figs, nor of a bramble bush
45 gather they grapes. The good man out of the
good treasure of his heart bringeth forth that
which is good; and the evil man out of the evil
treasure bringeth forth that which is evil: for
out of the abundance of the heart his mouth
speaketh.
46   And why call ye me, Lord, Lord, and do   =Mt. vii. 21
47 not the things which I say? Every one that   =Mt. vii.
  24–7

    [1] I.e. the loose garment above the girdle used as a
pocket.   [2] Or splinter.

cometh unto me, and heareth my words, and
doeth them, I will shew you to whom he is
48 like: he is like a man building a house, who
digged and went deep, and laid a foundation
upon the rock: and when a flood arose, the
stream brake against that house, and could
not shake it: because it had been well builded.
49 But he that heareth, and doeth not, is like a
man that built a house upon the earth without
a foundation; against which the stream brake,
and straightway it fell in; and the ruin of that
house was great.

II. THE RESPONSE
(cf. p. 86 and Jn. iv. 46–53)

A. THE CENTURION'S FAITH[1]

Mt. viii. 5   When Jesus was entered into Capernaum,   =Lk. vii.
there came unto him a centurion, beseeching   1–9
6 him, and saying, Lord, my servant lieth in the
house sick of the palsy, grievously tormented.
7 And he saith unto him, I will come and heal
8 him. And the centurion answered and said,
Lord, I am not worthy that thou shouldest
come under my roof: but only say the word,
9 and my servant shall be healed. For I also am
a man under authority, having under myself
soldiers: and I say to this one, Go, and he
goeth; and to another, Come, and he cometh;

[1] The Version in Mt. is probably nearer to the
original source.

and to my servant, Do this, and he doeth it.

10 And when Jesus heard it, he marvelled, and said to them that followed, Verily I say unto you, I have not found so great faith, no, not in Israel.

B. John the Baptist's Questioning
(cf. pp. 58, 86)

k. vii. 19   And John calling unto him two of his =Mt. xi.
disciples sent them to the Lord, saying, Art 2–11
thou he that cometh, or look we for another?

22 And Jesus answered and said unto them, Go your way, and tell John what things ye have seen and heard; the blind receive their sight, the lame walk, the lepers are cleansed, and the deaf hear, the dead are raised up, the poor have good tidings preached to them.

23 And blessed is he, whosoever shall find none occasion of stumbling in me.

24 And when the messengers of John were departed, he began to say unto the multitudes concerning John, What went ye out into the wilderness to behold? a reed shaken with the

25 wind? But what went ye out to see? a man clothed in soft raiment? Behold, they which are gorgeously apparelled, and live delicately,

26 are in kings' courts. But what went ye out to see? a prophet? Yea, I say unto you, and

27 much more than a prophet. This is he of whom it is written,

Behold, I send my messenger before thy
face,

Who shall prepare thy way before thee.

28 I say unto you, Among them that are born of
women there is none greater than John: yet
he that is but little in the kingdom of God is

29 greater than he. *And all the people when
they heard, and the publicans, justified God,
being baptized with the baptism of John.

30 But the Pharisees and the lawyers rejected for
themselves the counsel of God, being not

31 baptized of him.* Whereunto then shall I
liken the men of this generation, and to what

32 are they like? They are like unto children
that sit in the marketplace, and call one to
another; which say, We piped unto you, and
ye did not dance; we wailed, and ye did not

33 weep.[1] For John the Baptist is come eating
no bread nor drinking wine; and ye say, He

34 hath a devil. The Son of man is come eating
and drinking; and ye say, Behold, a gluttonous
man, and a winebibber, a friend of publicans

35 and sinners! And wisdom[2] is justified of all
her children.

*Not in ℳ
unless
Mt. xxi. 3

[1] I.e. the Jews complain that John will not dance
and Jesus will not weep.
[2] I.e. the Wisdom of God.

C. The Demands of Discipleship

Lk. ix. 57   A certain man said unto Jesus, I will follow =Mt. viii.
58 thee whithersoever thou goest. And Jesus 19–22
said unto him, The foxes have holes, and the
birds of the heaven have nests; but the Son
59 of man hath not where to lay his head. And
he said unto another, Follow me. But he
said, Lord, suffer me first to go and bury my
60 father. But he said unto him, Leave the dead
to bury their own dead; *but go thou and * Not in Mt.
61 publish abroad the kingdom of God. And
another also said, I will follow thee, Lord;
but first suffer me to bid farewell to them that
62 are at my house. But Jesus said unto him,
No man, having put his hand to the plough,
and looking back, is fit for the kingdom of
God.*

III. THE CLIMAX
(cf. pp. 92–4)

A. The Mission of the Disciples[1]

Lk. x. 2   And Jesus said unto the disciples, The har- =Mt. ix.
vest is plenteous, but the labourers are few: 37, 38;
pray ye therefore the Lord of the harvest, that x. 7–16
3 he send forth labourers into his harvest. Go

[1] For this section, usually called the Mission of
the Seventy, compare Mk. vi. 7–11 (Lk. ix. 1–5).
St Matthew combines the account here with that in
St Mark. Possibly the two refer to the same mission.

your ways: behold, I send you forth as lambs
4 in the midst of wolves. Carry no purse, no
wallet, no shoes: and salute no man on the
5 way. And into whatsoever house ye shall
6 enter, first say, Peace be to this house. And
if a son of peace be there, your peace shall rest
upon him: but if not, it shall turn to you again.
7 And in that same house remain, eating and
drinking such things as they give: for the
labourer is worthy of his hire. Go not from
8 house to house. And into whatsoever city ye
enter, and they receive you, eat such things
9 as are set before you: and heal the sick that
are therein, and say unto them, The kingdom
10 of God is come nigh unto you. But into
whatsoever city ye shall enter, and they
receive you not, go out into the streets thereof
11 and say, Even the dust from your city, that
cleaveth to our feet, we do wipe off against
you: howbeit know this, that the kingdom of
12 God is come nigh. I say unto you, It shall be
more tolerable in that day for Sodom, than
13 for that city. Woe unto thee, Chorazin! woe
unto thee, Bethsaida! for if the mighty works
had been done in Tyre and Sidon, which
were done in you, they would have repented
14 long ago, sitting in sackcloth and ashes. Howbeit it shall be more tolerable for Tyre and
15 Sidon in the judgement, than for you. And
thou, Capernaum, shalt thou be exalted unto
heaven? thou shalt be brought down unto

16 Hades. He that heareth you heareth me; and   =Mt. x. 40
he that receiveth me receiveth him that sent
me.

B. The Joy of the Lord
(cf. p. 62)

k. x.   21   In that same hour Jesus rejoiced, and said,   =Mt. xi.
I thank thee, O Father, Lord of heaven and   25‑7
earth, that thou didst hide these things from
the wise and understanding, and didst reveal
them unto babes: yea, Father; for so it was
22 well-pleasing in thy sight. All things have
been delivered unto me of my Father: and
no one knoweth who the Son is, save the
Father; and who the Father is, save the Son,
and he to whomsoever the Son willeth to
reveal him.[1]

t. xi.   28   *Come unto me, all ye that labour and are   * Not in Lk.
29 heavy laden, and I will give you rest. Take
my yoke upon you, and learn of me; for I am
meek and lowly in heart: and ye shall find
30 rest unto your souls. For my yoke is easy,
and my burden is light.*

k. x.   23   Blessed are the eyes which see the things   =Mt. xiii.
24 that ye see: for I say unto you, that many   16‑17
prophets and kings desired to see the things
which ye see, and saw them not; and to hear
the things which ye hear, and heard them not.

[1] This verse is very similar to many in the Fourth
Gospel: e.g. Jn. iii. 35, vi. 46, viii. 19, etc.

C. Concerning Prayer

Lk. xi. 2   When ye pray, say, Father, Hallowed be   =Mt. vi.
        3   thy name. Thy kingdom come. Give us day   9–13
        4   by day our daily bread. And forgive us our
            sins; for we ourselves also forgive every one
            that is indebted to us. And bring us not into
            temptation.

        9   And I say unto you, Ask, and it shall be   =Mt. vii.
            given you; seek, and ye shall find; knock, and   7–11
       10   it shall be opened unto you. For every one
            that asketh receiveth; and he that seeketh
            findeth; and to him that knocketh it shall be
       11   opened. And of which of you that is a father
            shall his son ask a loaf, and he give him a
            stone? or a fish, and he for a fish give him a
       12   serpent? Or if he shall ask an egg, will he
       13   give him a scorpion? If ye then, being evil,
            know how to give good gifts unto your
            children, how much more shall your heavenly
            Father give good things[1] to them that ask
            him?

IV. THE CONFLICT
(cf. pp. 57–8, 84–8)

A. The Causes of Rejection

Lk. xi. 14   Jesus was casting out a devil which was   =Mt. ix.
            dumb. And it came to pass, when the devil   32–4 and
            was gone out, the dumb man spake; and the   xii. 22–4

            [1] So Mt.: Lk. has "Holy Spirit".

15 multitudes marvelled. [1]But some of them said,
By Beelzebub the prince of the devils casteth

17 he out devils. But he, knowing their thoughts,
said unto them, Every kingdom divided
against itself is brought to desolation; and a

18 house divided against a house falleth. And
if Satan also is divided against himself, how
shall his kingdom stand? because ye say that

19 I cast out devils by Beelzebub. And if I by
Beelzebub cast out devils, by whom do your

20 sons cast them out? therefore shall they be
your judges. But if I by the finger of God
cast out devils, then is the kingdom of God

21 come upon you. When the strong man fully
armed[2] guardeth his own court, his goods are

22 in peace: but when a stronger than he shall
come upon him, and overcome him, he
taketh from him his whole armour wherein

23 he trusted, and divideth his spoils. He that is
not with me is against me; and he that

24 gathereth not with me scattereth.[3] The unclean spirit when he is gone out of the man,
passeth through waterless places, seeking
rest; and finding none, he saith, I will turn

25 back unto my house whence I came out. And
when he is come, he findeth it swept and

26 garnished. Then goeth he, and taketh to him

=Mt. xii. 25–6; cf. Mk. iii. 23–6

=Mt. xii. 27–9

=Mt. xii. 30

=Mt. xii. 43–5

---

[1] Cf. Mk. iii. 22–30.
[2] I.e. Satan, cf. Mk. iii. 27 and the similar image in Isaiah xlix. 24–6. Mt. replaces these two verses by the Marcan version.
[3] Cf. Mk. ix. 40 note.

seven other spirits more evil than himself; and they enter in and dwell there: and the last state of that man becometh worse than the first.

_{Lk. xi.} 29 And when others sought of him a sign from heaven, he began to say, This generation is an evil generation: it seeketh after a sign; and there shall no sign be given to it but the sign 30 of Jonah.[1] For even as Jonah became a sign unto the Ninevites, so shall also the Son of 31 man be to this generation. The queen of the south shall rise up in the judgement with the men of this generation, and shall condemn them: for she came from the ends of the earth to hear the wisdom of Solomon; and behold, 32 a greater than Solomon is here. The men of Nineveh shall stand up in the judgement with this generation, and shall condemn it: for they repented at the preaching of Jonah; and behold, a greater than Jonah is here.

= Mt. xii. 38–9, 41–2

33 No man, when he hath lighted a lamp, putteth it in a cellar, neither under the bushel, but on the stand, that they which enter in may 34 see the light.[2] The lamp of thy body is thine eye: when thine eye is single, thy whole body also is full of light; but when it is evil, thy 35 body also is full of darkness. Look therefore whether the light that is in thee be not darkness.

=Mt. vi. 22–3

[1] In Lk. evidently the preaching, not as in Mt. the three days and three nights in the belly of the whale.
[2] Cf. Mk. iv. 21.

B. The Rebuking of the Pharisees

xi. 39   Now do ye Pharisees cleanse the outside of   =Mt. xxiii.
           the cup and of the platter; but your inward   25
           part is full of extortion and wickedness.

     42   But woe unto you Pharisees! for ye tithe   =Mt. xxiii.
           mint and rue and every herb, and pass over   23
           judgement and the love of God: but these
           ought ye to have done, and not to leave the
     43   other undone. Woe unto you Pharisees! for   =Mt. xiii. 6,
           ye love the chief seats in the synagogues, and   7; cf. Mk. xii.
                                                             38–9
     44   the salutations in the marketplaces. Woe unto   =Mt. xxiii.
           you! for ye are as the tombs which appear not,   27
           and the men that walk over them know it not.

     46   Woe unto you lawyers also! for ye lade men   = Mt. xxiii. 4
           with burdens grievous to be borne, and ye
           yourselves touch not the burdens with one
     47   of your fingers. Woe unto you! for ye build   = Mt. xxiii.
           the tombs of the prophets, and your fathers   29–31
     48   killed them. So ye are witnesses and consent
           unto the works of your fathers: for they killed
     49   them, and ye build their tombs. Therefore   =Mt. xxiii.
           also said the wisdom of God, I will send unto   34–6
           them prophets and apostles; and some of
     50   them they shall kill and persecute; that the
           blood of all the prophets, which was shed
           from the foundation of the world, may be
     51   required of this generation; from the blood
           of Abel unto the blood of Zachariah,[1] who

---

[1] Cf. Gen. iv. 8 and 2 Chron. xxiv. 20–1, the first
and last murders recorded in the Old Testament.

perished between the altar and the sanctuary:
yea, I say unto you, it shall be required of this
52 generation.[1] Woe unto you lawyers! for ye   =Mt. xx
took away the key of knowledge: ye entered   13
not in yourselves, and them that were entering
in ye hindered.

C. The Encouraging of the Disciples

Lk. xii. 2   But there is nothing covered up, that shall   =Mt. x.
not be revealed: and hid, that shall not be   26–33
3 known. Wherefore whatsoever ye have said
in the darkness shall be heard in the light; and
what ye have spoken in the ear in the inner
chambers shall be proclaimed upon the
4 housetops. And I say unto you my friends,
Be not afraid of them which kill the body, and
5 after that have no more that they can do. But
I will warn you whom ye shall fear: Fear him,
which after he hath killed hath power to cast
6 into hell; yea, I say unto you, Fear him. Are
not five sparrows sold for two farthings[2]?
and not one of them is forgotten in the sight
7 of God. But the very hairs of your head are
all numbered. Fear not: ye are of more value
8 than many sparrows. And I say unto you,
Every one who shall confess me before men,

[1] Mt. has "All these things shall come upon this
generation".
[2] I.e. assarion or eight lepta (mites; cf. Lk. xii. 59).

him shall the Son of man also confess before
9 the angels of God: but he that denieth me in
the presence of men shall be denied in the
10 presence of the angels of God. And every one
who shall speak a word against the Son of
man, it shall be forgiven him: but unto him
that blasphemeth against the Holy Spirit it
11 shall not be forgiven.[1] And when they bring =Mt. x.
you before the synagogues, and the rulers, 19–20
and the authorities, be not anxious how or
what ye shall answer, or what ye shall say:
12 for the Holy Spirit shall teach you in that
very hour what ye ought to say.[2]

22   Therefore I say unto you, Be not anxious =Mt. vi.
for your life, what ye shall eat; nor yet for 25–33
23 your body, what ye shall put on. For the life
is more than the food, and the body than the
24 raiment. Consider the ravens, that they sow
not, neither reap; which have no store-
chamber nor barn; and God feedeth them:
of how much more value are ye than the
25 birds! And which of you by being anxious
26 can add a cubit unto his stature? If then ye
are not able to do even that which is least,
why are ye anxious concerning the rest?
27 Consider the lilies, how they grow: they toil
not, neither do they spin; yet I say unto you,
Even Solomon in all his glory was not arrayed
28 like one of these. But if God doth so clothe

[1] Cf. Mk. iii. 28–9: Mt. xii. 31–2 follows Mk.
[2] Cf. Mk. xiii. 11.

the grass in the field, which to-day is, and
to-morrow is cast into the oven; how much
more shall he clothe you, O ye of little faith?

29 And seek not ye what ye shall eat, and what
ye shall drink, neither be ye of doubtful

30 mind. For all these things do the nations
of the world seek after: but your Father
knoweth that ye have need of these things.

31 Howbeit seek ye his kingdom, and these

32 things shall be added unto you. Fear not,
little flock; for it is your Father's good

33 pleasure to give you the kingdom. Sell that
ye have, and give alms; make for yourselves
purses which wax not old, a treasure in the
heavens that faileth not, where no thief

34 draweth near, neither moth destroyeth. For
where your treasure is, there will your heart
be also.

39 But know this, that if the master of the
house had known in what hour the thief was
coming, he would have watched, and not

40 have left his house to be broken through. Be
ye also ready: for in an hour that ye think not
the Son of man cometh.

42 Who then is the faithful and wise steward,
whom his lord shall set over his household,
to give them their portion of food in due

43 season? Blessed is that servant, whom his

44 lord when he cometh shall find so doing. Of
a truth I say unto you, that he will set him

45 over all that he hath. But if that servant shall

This one
verse (i.e.
is not in N
=Mt. vi.
20–1

=Mt. xxi
43–51

say in his heart, My lord delayeth his coming; and shall begin to beat the menservants and the maidservants, and to eat and drink, and
46 to be drunken; the lord of that servant shall come in a day when he expecteth not, and in an hour when he knoweth not, and shall cut him asunder, and appoint his portion with the unfaithful.

51   Think ye that I am come to give peace in the earth? I tell you, Nay; but rather division: =Mt. x. 34–6
52 for there shall be from henceforth five in one house divided, three against two, and two
53 against three. They shall be divided, father against son, and son against father; mother against daughter, and daughter against her mother; mother in law against her daughter in law, and daughter in law against her mother in law.

58   For as thou art going with thine adversary before the magistrate, on the way give =Mt. v. 25–6 diligence to be quit of him; lest haply he hale thee unto the judge, and the judge shall deliver thee to the officer, and the officer shall
59 cast thee into prison. I say unto thee, Thou shalt by no means come out thence, till thou have paid the very last mite.[1]

[1] I.e. lepton, half a quadrans, eighth of an assarion.

V. THE JUDGEMENT

A. The Growth of the Kingdom
(cf. p. 88)

Lk. xiii. 18
19   Unto what is the kingdom of God like? and whereunto shall I liken it?[1] It is like unto a grain of mustard seed,[2] which a man took, and cast into his own garden; and it grew, and became a tree; and the birds of the
20 heaven lodged in the branches thereof. And again he said, Whereunto shall I liken the
21 kingdom of God? It is like unto leaven, which a woman took and hid in three measures of meal, till it was all leavened.

    =Mt. xiii

B. The Two Ways
(cf. pp. 86–7, 96)

Lk. xiii. 24
    Strive to enter in by the narrow door: for many, I say unto you, shall seek to enter in,
25 and shall not be able. When once the master of the house is risen up, and hath shut to the door, and ye begin to stand without, and to knock at the door, saying, Lord, open to us; and he shall answer and say to you, I know
26 you not whence ye are; then shall ye begin to say, We did eat and drink in thy presence,

    This sec is perha composite Mt. vii. 14, 21–3; 11, 12 close to it

---

[1] Cf. Mk. iv. 30–2; Mt. xiii. 31–2 follows Mk.
[2] Probably not our mustard but the *Salvadora persica*, a large shrub.

27 and thou didst teach in our streets; and he
shall say, I tell you, I know not whence ye are;
depart from me, all ye workers of iniquity.

28 There shall be the weeping and gnashing of
teeth, when ye shall see Abraham, and Isaac,
and Jacob, and all the prophets, in the kingdom of God, and yourselves cast forth

29 without. And they shall come from the east
and west, and from the north and south, and

30 shall sit down in the kingdom of God. And
behold, there are last which shall be first,
and there are first which shall be last.

34   O Jerusalem, Jerusalem, which killeth the   = Mt. xxiii.
prophets, and stoneth them that are sent   37–9
unto her! how often would I have gathered
thy children together, even as a hen gathereth
her own brood under her wings, and ye

35 would not! Behold, your house is left unto
you desolate: and I say unto you, Ye shall not
see me, until ye shall say, Blessed is he that
cometh in the name of the Lord.

Lk. xiv. 1   And it came to pass, when he went into the   Mt. xii. 9–14
house of one of the rulers of the Pharisees on   conflates this
a sabbath to eat bread, that they were watching   passage with
Mk. iii. 1–6.

2 him. And behold, there was before him a   Cf. also Lk.
xiii. 10–17

3 certain man which had the dropsy. And Jesus
answering spake unto the lawyers and Pharisees, saying, Is it lawful to heal on the sabbath,

4 or not? But they held their peace. And he
took him, and healed him, and let him go.

5 And he said unto them, Which of you shall

have an ass[1] or an ox fallen into a well, and
will not straightway draw him up on a sabbath
6 day? And they could not answer again unto
these things.

11   Every one that exalteth himself shall be   =Mt.xxiii.
humbled; and he that humbleth himself shall
be exalted.

26   If any man cometh unto me, and hateth not   =Mt. x. 37
his own father, and mother, and wife, and
children, and brethren, and sisters, yea, and
his own life also, he cannot be my disciple.

27 Whosoever doth not bear his own cross, and
come after me, cannot be my disciple.

34   Salt therefore is good: but if even the salt   =Mt. v. 13
have lost its savour, wherewith shall it be
35 seasoned?[2] It is fit neither for the land nor
for the dunghill: men cast it out. He that
hath ears to hear, let him hear.

Lk. xvi. 13   No servant can serve two masters: for   =Mt. vi. 2
either he will hate the one, and love the other;
or else he will hold to one, and despise the
other. Ye cannot serve God and mammon.

16   The law and the prophets were until John: =Mt. xi.
from that time the gospel of the kingdom of   12–13
God is preached, and every man entereth
17 violently into it.[3] But it is easier for heaven   =Mt. v. 18
and earth to pass away, than for one tittle of

[1] The most important MSS. read "a son".
[2] Cf. Mk. ix. 50.
[3] Mt.'s version seems to mean "do violence to it",
i.e. persecute, cf. p. 21.

18 the law to fall. Every one that putteth away = Mt. v. 32;
his wife, and marrieth another, committeth cf. Mk. x. 11,
adultery: and he that marrieth one that is put 12
away from a husband committeth adultery.

C. The Challenge to Decision

k. xvii. 1   It is impossible but that occasions of = Mt. xviii. 7
stumbling should come: but woe unto him,
2 through whom they come! It were well for
him if a millstone were hanged about his neck,
and he were thrown into the sea, rather than
that he should cause one of these little ones
3 to stumble. Take heed to yourselves: if thy = Mt. xviii.
brother sin, rebuke him; and if he repent, 15
4 forgive him. And if he sin against thee seven = Mt. xviii.
times in the day, and seven times turn again 22
to thee, saying, I repent; thou shalt forgive
him.
6   If ye have faith as a grain of mustard seed, = Mt. xvii.
ye would say unto this sycamine tree,[1] Be 20
thou rooted up, and be thou planted in the
sea; and it would have obeyed you.
22   *The days will come, when ye shall desire * Not in Mt.
to see one of the days of the Son of man, and
23 ye shall not see it.* And they shall say to you, = Mt. xxiv.
Lo, there! Lo, here! go not away, nor follow 23; cf. Mk.
xiii. 21
24 after them: for as the lightning, when it = Mt. xxiv.
lighteneth out of the one part under the 27

[1] I.e. a mulberry or possibly a fig as in Lk. xix. 4.

heaven, shineth unto the other part under heaven; so shall the Son of man be in his day.

25 But first must he suffer many things and be
26 rejected of this generation. And as it came = Mt. xxiv
to pass in the days of Noah, even so shall it be 37-9
27 also in the days of the Son of man. They ate, they drank, they married, they were given in marriage, until the day that Noah entered into the ark, and the flood came, and de-
31 stroyed them all. *In that day, he which shall * Not in M
be on the housetop, and his goods in the house, For this ve
let him not go down to take them away: and cf. Mk. x
let him that is in the field likewise not return 15, 16
33 back.* Whosoever shall seek to gain his life = Mt. x. 3
shall lose it: but whosoever shall lose his life
34 shall preserve it.[1] I say unto you, In that = Mt. xxiv
night there shall be two men on one bed; the 40-1
one shall be taken, and the other shall be left.
35 There shall be two women grinding together; the one shall be taken, and the other shall be
37 left. Where the body is, thither will the eagles[2] = Mt. xxiv
also be gathered together. 28

[1] Cf. Mk. viii. 35.
[2] Or vultures; i.e. where there is spiritual death, there will be destruction: perhaps a special allusion to the corruption of Judaism and the eagles of Rome.

The Gospel contained only in that according to St Luke[1]

I. THE BIRTH AND CHILDHOOD OF JESUS

1 Forasmuch as many have taken in hand to draw up a [1] narrative concerning those matters which have been fulfilled among us, even as they delivered them unto [2] us, which from the beginning were eyewitnesses and ministers of the word, it seemed good to me also, having [3] traced the course of all things accurately from the first, to write unto thee in order, most excellent Theophilus; that thou mightest know the certainty concerning the [4] things wherein thou wast instructed.

There was in the days of Herod,[2] king of Judæa, a [5] certain priest named Zacharias, of the course of Abijah:[3] and he had a wife of the daughters of Aaron, and her name was Elisabeth. And they were both righteous [6] before God, walking in all the commandments and ordinances of the Lord blameless. And they had no [7] child, because that Elisabeth was barren, and they both were now well stricken in years.

[1] A few additional details are found in other parts of our Third Gospel, especially in ch. xxi. The Passion narrative though incorporating much from St Mark is largely independent and is here printed in full.

[2] Cf. p. 9. Mt. ii. 1, etc. also places the nativity in Herod's reign, i.e. before 4 B.C.

[3] Cf. 1 Chron. xxiv. 10.

8   Now it came to pass, while he executed the priest's
9 office before God in the order of his course, according to
the custom of the priest's office, his lot was to enter into
10 the temple of the Lord and burn incense. And the whole
multitude of the people were praying without at the hour
11 of incense. And there appeared unto him an angel of the
Lord[1] standing on the right side of the altar of incense.
12 And Zacharias was troubled when he saw him, and fear
13 fell upon him. But the angel said unto him, Fear not,
Zacharias: because thy supplication is heard, and thy wife
Elisabeth shall bear thee a son, and thou shalt call his
14 name John. And thou shalt have joy and gladness; and
15 many shall rejoice at his birth. For he shall be great in
the sight of the Lord, and he shall drink no wine nor
strong drink; and he shall be filled with the Holy Ghost,
16 even from his mother's womb. And many of the children
17 of Israel shall he turn unto the Lord their God. And he
shall go before his face in the spirit and power of Elijah,[2]
to turn the hearts of the fathers to the children, and the
disobedient to walk in the wisdom of the just; to make
18 ready for the Lord a people prepared for him. And
Zacharias said unto the angel, Whereby shall I know
this? for I am an old man, and my wife well stricken in
19 years. And the angel answering said unto him, I am
Gabriel,[3] that stand in the presence of God; and I was
sent to speak unto thee, and to bring thee these good
20 tidings. And behold, thou shalt be silent and not able to

---

[1] References to angels are characteristic of this Evangelist, and perhaps indicate that he was a Greek. For another mode of revelation cf. Mt. i. 20, ii. 12.

[2] Cf. Mk. ix. 13.

[3] I.e. "Man of God": for the name cf. Dan. viii. 16.

speak, until the day that these things shall come to pass, because thou believedst not my words, which shall be fulfilled in their season. And the people were waiting for 21 Zacharias, and they marvelled while he tarried in the temple. And when he came out, he could not speak unto 22 them: and they perceived that he had seen a vision in the temple: and he continued making signs unto them, and remained dumb. And it came to pass, when the days of 23 his ministration were fulfilled, he departed unto his house.

And after these days Elisabeth his wife conceived; and 24 she hid herself five months, saying, Thus hath the Lord 25 done unto me in the days wherein he looked upon me, to take away my reproach among men.

Now in the sixth month the angel Gabriel was sent 26 from God unto a city of Galilee, named Nazareth, to a 27 virgin betrothed to a man whose name was Joseph, of the house of David; and the virgin's name was Mary. And 28 he came in unto her, and said, Hail, thou that art highly favoured, the Lord is with thee. But she was greatly 29 troubled at the saying, and cast in her mind what manner of salutation this might be. And the angel said unto her, 30 Fear not, Mary: for thou hast found favour with God. And behold, thou shalt conceive in thy womb, and bring 31 forth a son, and shalt call his name JESUS. He shall be 32 great, and shall be called the Son of the Most High: and the Lord God shall give unto him the throne of his father David: and he shall reign over the house of Jacob for 33 ever; and of his kingdom there shall be no end. And 34 Mary said unto the angel, How shall this be, seeing I know not a man? And the angel answered and said unto 35

her, The Holy Ghost shall come upon thee, and the power of the Most High shall overshadow thee: wherefore also that which is to be born shall be called holy, the Son of
36 God. And behold, Elisabeth thy kinswoman, she also hath conceived a son in her old age: and this is the sixth
37 month with her that was called barren. For no word from
38 God shall be void of power. And Mary said, Behold, the handmaid of the Lord; be it unto me according to thy word. And the angel departed from her.

39 And Mary arose in these days and went into the hill
40 country with haste, into a city of Judah; and entered into
41 the house of Zacharias and saluted Elisabeth. And it came to pass, when Elisabeth heard the salutation of
42 Mary, the babe leaped in her womb; and Elisabeth was filled with the Holy Ghost; and she lifted up her voice
43 with a loud cry, and said, Blessed art thou among women, and blessed is the fruit of thy womb. And whence is this
44 to me, that the mother of my Lord should come unto me?
45 For behold, when the voice of thy salutation came into mine ears, the babe leaped in my womb for joy. And blessed is she that believed; for there shall be a fulfilment of the things which have been spoken to her from the
46 Lord. And Mary said,[1]

My soul doth magnify the Lord,

47 And my spirit hath rejoiced in God my Saviour.

48 For he hath looked upon the low estate of his hand-
maiden:

[1] The Magnificat is full of the language of the Old Testament. Cf. especially the Song of Hannah, 1 Sam. ii. 1–10. The composition of such sequences, based upon scriptural phrases, seems to have been usual in Jewish life at this time: such a sequence is found in Rom. iii. 10–18.

For behold, from henceforth all generations shall call
me blessed.

For he that is mighty hath done to me great things; 49
And holy is his name.

And his mercy is unto generations and generations 50
On them that fear him.

He hath shewed strength with his arm; 51
He hath scattered the proud in the imagination of
their heart.

He hath put down princes from their thrones, 52
And hath exalted them of low degree.

The hungry he hath filled with good things; 53
And the rich he hath sent empty away.

He hath holpen Israel his servant, 54
That he might remember mercy

(As he spake unto our fathers) 55
Toward Abraham and his seed for ever.

And Mary abode with her about three months, and 56
returned unto her house.

Now Elisabeth's time was fulfilled that she should be 57
delivered; and she brought forth a son. And her neigh- 58
bours and her kinsfolk heard that the Lord had magnified
his mercy towards her; and they rejoiced with her. And 59
it came to pass on the eighth day, that they came to cir-
cumcise the child; and they would have called him
Zacharias, after the name of his father. And his mother 60
answered and said, Not so; but he shall be called John.
And they said unto her, There is none of thy kindred that 61
is called by this name. And they made signs to his father, 62
what he would have him called. And he asked for a 63
writing tablet, and wrote, saying, His name is John. And

64 they marvelled all. And his mouth was opened immediately, and his tongue loosed, and he spake, blessing
65 God. And fear came on all that dwelt round about them:
and all these sayings were noised abroad throughout all
66 the hill country of Judæa. And all that heard them laid
them up in their heart, saying, What then shall this child
be? For the hand of the Lord was with him.

67   And his father Zacharias was filled with the Holy
Ghost, and prophesied, saying,

68   Blessed be the Lord, the God of Israel;
    For he hath visited and wrought redemption for his
        people,
69   And hath raised up a horn of salvation for us
    In the house of his servant David
70   (As he spake by the mouth of his holy prophets
        which have been since the world began),
71   Salvation from our enemies, and from the hand of
        all that hate us;
72   To shew mercy towards our fathers,
    And to remember his holy covenant;
73   The oath which he sware unto Abraham our father,
74   To grant unto us that we being delivered out of the
        hand of our enemies
    Should serve him without fear,
75   In holiness and righteousness before him all our days.
76   Yea and thou, child, shalt be called the prophet of
        the Most High:
    For thou shalt go before the face of the Lord to
        make ready his ways;
77   To give knowledge of salvation unto his people
    In the remission of their sins,

Because of the tender mercy of our God,   78
Whereby the dayspring from on high shall visit us,
To shine upon them that sit in darkness and the   79
    shadow of death;
To guide our feet into the way of peace.

And the child grew, and waxed strong in spirit, and   80
was in the deserts till the day of his shewing unto Israel.[1]

2 Now it came to pass in those days, there went out a decree   1
from Cæsar Augustus, that all the world should be
enrolled. This was the first enrolment made when   2
Quirinius was governor of Syria.[2] And all went to enrol   3
themselves, every one to his own city. And Joseph also   4
went up from Galilee, out of the city of Nazareth, into
Judæa, to the city of David, which is called Bethlehem,
because he was of the house and family of David; to   5
enrol himself with Mary, who was betrothed to him,
being great with child. And it came to pass, while they   6
were there, the days were fulfilled that she should be
delivered. And she brought forth her firstborn son; and   7
she wrapped him in swaddling clothes, and laid him in
a manger, because there was no room for them in the inn.

And there were shepherds in the same country abiding   8
in the field, and keeping watch by night over their flock.
And an angel of the Lord stood by them, and the glory   9
of the Lord shone round about them: and they were sore
afraid. And the angel said unto them, Be not afraid; for   10
behold, I bring you good tidings of great joy which shall

---

[1] I.e. of his public ministry, cf. iii. 2.
[2] Q. was legatus and held the census mentioned in Acts v. 37 in
A.D. 6. He was in Syria earlier for a campaign and may have
initiated a census in 8–6 B.C. Cf. p. 10.

11 be to all the people: for there is born to you this day in the
12 city of David a Saviour, which is Christ the Lord. And
this is the sign unto you; Ye shall find a babe wrapped in
13 swaddling clothes, and lying in a manger. And suddenly
there was with the angel a multitude of the heavenly host
praising God, and saying,

14   Glory to God in the highest,
     And on earth peace among men in whom he is well
        pleased.

15   And it came to pass, when the angels went away from
them into heaven, the shepherds said one to another,
Let us now go even unto Bethlehem, and see this thing
that is come to pass, which the Lord hath made known
16 unto us. And they came with haste, and found both Mary
17 and Joseph, and the babe lying in the manger. And when
they saw it, they made known concerning the saying
18 which was spoken to them about this child. And all that
heard it wondered at the things which were spoken unto
19 them by the shepherds. But Mary kept all these sayings,
20 pondering them in her heart. And the shepherds returned, glorifying and praising God for all the things that
they had heard and seen, even as it was spoken unto them.

21   And when eight days were fulfilled for circumcising
him, his name was called JESUS, which was so called by
the angel before he was conceived in the womb.

22   And when the days of their purification according to
the law of Moses were fulfilled,[1] they brought him up to
23 Jerusalem, to present him to the Lord (as it is written in
the law of the Lord, Every male that openeth the womb
24 shall be called holy to the Lord), and to offer a sacrifice

[1] Forty days after birth; cf. Levit. xii. 2–4.

according to that which is said in the law of the Lord,
A pair of turtledoves, or two young pigeons. And behold, 25
there was a man in Jerusalem, whose name was Simeon;
and this man was righteous and devout, looking for the
consolation of Israel:[1] and the Holy Spirit was upon him.
And it had been revealed unto him by the Holy Spirit, 26
that he should not see death, before he had seen the
Lord's Christ. And he came in the Spirit into the temple: 27
and when the parents brought in the child Jesus, that
they might do concerning him after the custom of the
law, then he received him into his arms, and blessed God, 28
and said,

Now lettest thou thy servant depart, O Lord, 29
According to thy word, in peace;
For mine eyes have seen thy salvation, 30
Which thou hast prepared before the face of all 31
peoples;
A light for revelation to the Gentiles, 32
And the glory of thy people Israel.

And his father and his mother were marvelling at the 33
things which were spoken concerning him; and Simeon 34
blessed them, and said unto Mary his mother, Behold,
this child is set for the falling and rising up[2] of many in
Israel; and for a sign which is spoken against; yea and 35
a sword shall pierce through thine own soul; that
thoughts out of many hearts may be revealed. And there 36
was one Anna, a prophetess, the daughter of Phanuel, of
the tribe of Asher (she was of a great age, having lived
with a husband seven years from her virginity, and she 37

[1] I.e. the Messiah; cf. Mk. xv. 43 of Joseph of Arimathæa.
[2] I.e. his coming involves a decision—hostility or discipleship.

had been a widow even for fourscore and four years),
which departed not from the temple, worshipping with
38 fastings and supplications night and day. And coming
up at that very hour she gave thanks unto God, and
spake of him to all them that were looking for the
39 redemption of Jerusalem. And when they had accomplished all things that were according to the law of
the Lord, they returned into Galilee, to their own city
Nazareth.

40　And the child grew, and waxed strong, filled with
wisdom: and the grace of God was upon him.

41　And his parents went every year to Jerusalem at the
42 feast of the passover. And when he was twelve years old,
43 they went up after the custom of the feast; and when they
had fulfilled the days, as they were returning, the boy
Jesus tarried behind in Jerusalem; and his parents knew
44 it not; but supposing him to be in the company, they
went a day's journey; and they sought for him among
45 their kinsfolk and acquaintance: and when they found
him not, they returned to Jerusalem, seeking for him.
46 And it came to pass, after three days they found him in
the temple, sitting in the midst of the doctors, both
47 hearing them, and asking them questions: and all that
heard him were amazed at his understanding and his
48 answers. And when they saw him, they were astonished:
and his mother said unto him, Son, why hast thou thus
dealt with us? behold, thy father and I sought thee
49 sorrowing. And he said unto them, How is it that ye
sought me? wist ye not that I must be in my Father's
50 house? And they understood not the saying which he
51 spake unto them. And he went down with them, and

came to Nazareth; and he was subject unto them: and his mother kept all these sayings in her heart.

And Jesus advanced in wisdom and stature, and in 52 favour with God and men.

II. THE BAPTISM
(cf. Mk. i. 1–11; Q, pp. 163–4)

3 Now in the fifteenth year of the reign of Tiberius 1 Cæsar,[1] Pontius Pilate being governor of Judæa, and Herod being tetrarch of Galilee, and his brother Philip tetrarch of the region of Ituræa and Trachonitis, and Lysanias tetrarch of Abilene, in the high-priesthood of 2 Annas and Caiaphas,[2] the word of God came unto John the son of Zacharias in the wilderness. And he came into 3 all the region round about Jordan, preaching the baptism of repentance unto remission of sins; as it is written in 4 the book of the words of Isaiah the prophet,[3]

The voice of one crying in the wilderness,
Make ye ready the way of the Lord,
Make his paths straight.
Every valley shall be filled, 5
And every mountain and hill shall be brought low;
And the crooked shall become straight,
And the rough ways smooth;
And all flesh shall see the salvation of God. 6

And the multitudes asked him, saying, What then must 10 we do? And he answered and said unto them, He that 11 hath two coats, let him impart to him that hath none; and

---

[1] I.e. A.D. 28–9.
[2] Cf. p. 19.　　　　　[3] Is. xl. 3–5.

12 he that hath food, let him do likewise. And there came
also publicans to be baptized, and they said unto him,
13 Master, what must we do? And he said unto them,
14 Extort no more than that which is appointed you. And
soldiers also asked him, saying, And we, what must we
do? And he said unto them, Do violence to no man,
neither exact anything wrongfully; and be content with
your wages.

18 With many other exhortations therefore preached he
19 good tidings unto the people; but Herod the tetrarch,
being reproved by him for Herodias his brother's wife,
20 and for all the evil things which Herod had done, added
yet this above all, that he shut up John in prison.

23 And Jesus himself, when he began to teach, was about
thirty years of age, being the son (as was supposed) of
Joseph, the son of Heli.[1]

III. THE PREACHING AT NAZARETH
(cf. p. 54)

4 14 And Jesus returned in the power of the Spirit into
Galilee: and a fame went out concerning him through all
15 the region round about. And he taught in their synagogues, being glorified of all.

16 And he came to Nazareth, where he had been brought
up: and he entered, as his custom was, into the synagogue
17 on the sabbath day, and stood up to read. And there was
delivered unto him the book of the prophet Isaiah. And
he opened the book, and found the place where it was
written,[2]

---

[1] Here follows the genealogy.   [2] Is. lxi. 1, 2.

The Spirit of the Lord is upon me,   18
Because he anointed me to preach good tidings to the
    poor:
He hath sent me to proclaim release to the captives,
And recovering of sight to the blind,
To set at liberty them that are bruised,
To proclaim the acceptable year of the Lord.   19
And he closed the book, and gave it back to the attendant,   20
and sat down: and the eyes of all in the synagogue were
fastened on him. And he began to say unto them, To-day   21
hath this scripture been fulfilled in your ears. And all   22
bare him witness, and wondered at the words of grace
which proceeded out of his mouth: and they said, Is not
this Joseph's son? And he said unto them, Doubtless ye   23
will say unto me this parable, Physician, heal thyself:
whatsoever we have heard done at Capernaum, do also
here in thine own country. And he said, Verily I say   24
unto you, No prophet is acceptable in his own country.
But of a truth I say unto you, There were many widows   25
in Israel in the days of Elijah,[1] when the heaven was shut
up three years and six months, when there came a great
famine over all the land; and unto none of them was   26
Elijah sent, but only to Zarephath, in the land of Sidon,
unto a woman that was a widow. And there were many   27
lepers in Israel in the time of Elisha the prophet;[2] and
none of them was cleansed, but only Naaman the
Syrian. And they were all filled with wrath in the syna-   28
gogue, as they heard these things; and they rose up, and   29
cast him forth out of the city, and led him unto the brow
of the hill whereon their city was built,[3] that they might

---

[1] 1 Kings xvii. 8–xviii. 1.   [2] 2 Kings v. 1–14.   [3] Cf. p. 51.

30 throw him down headlong. But he passing through the midst of them went his way.

IV. WORKS OF POWER

A. Over Nature

5 1 Now it came to pass, while the multitude pressed upon him and heard the word of God, that he was standing by 2 the lake of Gennesaret; and he saw two boats standing by the lake: but the fishermen had gone out of them, and 3 were washing their nets. And he entered into one of the boats, which was Simon's, and asked him to put out a little from the land. And he sat down and taught the 4 multitudes out of the boat. And when he had left speaking, he said unto Simon, Put out into the deep, and 5 let down your nets for a draught. And Simon answered and said, Master, we toiled all night, and took nothing: 6 but at thy word I will let down the nets. And when they had this done, they inclosed a great multitude of fishes; 7 and their nets were breaking; and they beckoned unto their partners in the other boat, that they should come and help them. And they came, and filled both the boats, 8 so that they began to sink. But Simon Peter, when he saw it, fell down at Jesus' knees, saying, Depart from me; 9 for I am a sinful man, O Lord. For he was amazed, and all that were with him, at the draught of the fishes which 10 they had taken; and so were also James and John, sons of Zebedee, which were partners with Simon. And Jesus said unto Simon, Fear not; from henceforth thou shalt

catch men. And when they had brought their boats to 11
land, they left all, and followed him.

B. Over Death

7   And it came to pass soon afterwards, that he went to 11
a city called Nain; and his disciples went with him, and
a great multitude. Now when he drew near to the gate 12
of the city, behold, there was carried out one that was
dead, the only son of his mother, and she was a widow:
and much people of the city was with her. And when the 13
Lord saw her, he had compassion on her, and said unto
her, Weep not. And he came nigh and touched the bier: 14
and the bearers stood still. And he said, Young man, I say
unto thee, Arise. And he that was dead sat up, and began 15
to speak. And he gave him to his mother. And fear took 16
hold on all: and they glorified God, saying, A great
prophet is arisen among us: and, God hath visited his
people. And this report went forth concerning him in 17
the whole of Judæa, and all the region round about.

C. Over Sin

And one of the Pharisees desired him that he would eat 36
with him. And he entered into the Pharisee's house, and
sat down to meat.[1] And behold, a woman which was in 37
the city, a sinner; and when she knew that he was sitting
at meat in the Pharisee's house, she brought an alabaster

[1] This incident is similar to that in Mk. xiv. 3–9.

38 cruse of ointment, and standing behind at his feet, weeping, she began to wet his feet with her tears, and wiped them with the hair of her head, and kissed his feet,

39 and anointed them with the ointment. Now when the Pharisee which had bidden him saw it, he spake within himself, saying, This man, if he were a prophet, would have perceived who and what manner of woman this is

40 which toucheth him, that she is a sinner. And Jesus answering said unto him, Simon, I have somewhat to say

41 unto thee. And he saith, Master, say on. A certain lender had two debtors: the one owed five hundred pence, and

42 the other fifty. When they had not wherewith to pay, he forgave them both. Which of them therefore will love

43 him most? Simon answered and said, He, I suppose, to whom he forgave the most. And he said unto him, Thou

44 hast rightly judged. And turning to the woman, he said unto Simon, Seest thou this woman? I entered into thine house, thou gavest me no water for my feet: but she hath wetted my feet with her tears, and wiped them with her

45 hair. Thou gavest me no kiss: but she, since the time I

46 came in, hath not ceased to kiss my feet. My head with oil thou didst not anoint: but she hath anointed my feet

47 with ointment. Wherefore I say unto thee, Her sins, which are many, are forgiven; for she loved much: but

48 to whom little is forgiven, the same loveth little. And he

49 said unto her, Thy sins are forgiven. And they that sat at meat with him began to say within themselves, Who is

50 this that even forgiveth sins? And he said unto the woman, Thy faith hath saved thee; go in peace.

8 1 And it came to pass soon afterwards, that he went about through cities and villages, preaching and bringing

the good tidings of the kingdom of God, and with him
the twelve, and certain women which had been healed 2
of evil spirits and infirmities, Mary that was called
Magdalene, from whom seven devils had gone out, and 3
Joanna the wife of Chuza Herod's steward,[1] and Susanna,
and many others, which ministered unto them of their
substance.

V. LESSONS OF MERCY
(cf. p. 89)

A. TO THE DISCIPLES—IN SAMARIA

9   And it came to pass, when the days were well-nigh 51
come that he should be received up, he stedfastly set his
face to go to Jerusalem, and sent messengers before his 52
face: and they went, and entered into a village of the
Samaritans, to make ready for him. And they did not 53
receive him, because his face was as though he were
going to Jerusalem. And when his disciples James and 54
John saw this, they said, Lord, wilt thou that we bid fire
to come down from heaven, and consume them?[2] But 55
he turned, and rebuked them. And they went to another 56
village.

[1] Cf. xxiv. 10. Possibly the source of Lk.'s special knowledge of
Herod, cf. xiii. 31-3, xxiii. 7-12: or this may be due to Manaen,
Acts xiii. 1.
[2] As Elijah had done, 2 Kings i. 10.

B. To a Rabbi—The Good Samaritan

10 25　　And behold, a certain lawyer stood up and tempted him, saying, Master, what shall I do to inherit eternal
26 life? And he said unto him, What is written in the law?
27 how readest thou? And he answering said, Thou shalt love the Lord thy God with all thy heart, and with all thy soul, and with all thy strength, and with all thy mind; and
28 thy neighbour as thyself. And he said unto him, Thou
29 hast answered right: this do, and thou shalt live. But he, desiring to justify himself, said unto Jesus, And who is
30 my neighbour? Jesus made answer and said, A certain man was going down from Jerusalem to Jericho; and he fell among robbers, which both stripped him and beat
31 him, and departed, leaving him half dead. And by chance a certain priest was going down that way: and when he
32 saw him, he passed by on the other side. And in like manner a Levite also, when he came to the place, and saw
33 him, passed by on the other side. But a certain Samaritan, as he journeyed, came where he was: and when he saw
34 him, he was moved with compassion, and came to him, and bound up his wounds, pouring on them oil and wine; and he set him on his own beast, and brought him to an
35 inn, and took care of him. And on the morrow he took out two pence, and gave them to the host, and said, Take care of him; and whatsoever thou spendest more, I, when
36 I come back again, will repay thee. Which of these three, thinkest thou, proved neighbour unto him that fell
37 among the robbers? And he said, He that shewed mercy

on him. And Jesus said unto him, Go, and do thou likewise.

C. To Martha—The Good Part

Now as they went on their way, he entered into a 38 certain village: and a certain woman named Martha received him into her house. And she had a sister called 39 Mary, which also sat at the Lord's feet, and heard his word. But Martha was cumbered about much serving; 40 and she came up to him, and said, Lord, dost thou not care that my sister did leave me to serve alone? bid her therefore that she help me. But the Lord answered and 41 said unto her, Martha, Martha, thou art anxious and troubled about many things: but one thing is needful: 42 for Mary hath chosen the good part, which shall not be taken away from her.

D. Of Persistence
(cf. xviii. 1–8, and p. 94)

11 And it came to pass, as he was praying in a certain 1 place, that when he ceased, one of his disciples said unto him, Lord, teach us to pray, even as John also taught his disciples.

And he said unto them, Which of you shall have a 5 friend, and shall go unto him at midnight, and say to him, Friend, lend me three loaves; for a friend of mine is come 6 to me from a journey, and I have nothing to set before him; and he from within shall answer and say, Trouble 7

me not: the door is now shut, and my children are with
8 me in bed; I cannot rise and give thee? I say unto you,
Though he will not rise and give him, because he is his
friend, yet because of his importunity he will arise and
give him as many as he needeth.

VI. LESSONS OF WARNING
(cf. pp. 91–2)

A. AGAINST COVETOUSNESS—THE RICH FOOL

12 13   And one out of the multitude said unto him, Master,
14 bid my brother divide the inheritance with me. But he
said unto him, Man, who made me a judge or a divider
15 over you? And he said unto them, Take heed, and keep
yourselves from all covetousness: for a man's life con-
sisteth not in the abundance of the things which he
16 possesseth. And he spake a parable unto them, saying,
The ground of a certain rich man brought forth plenti-
17 fully: and he reasoned within himself, saying, What shall
18 I do, because I have not where to bestow my fruits? And
he said, This will I do: I will pull down my barns, and
build greater; and there will I bestow all my corn and my
19 goods. And I will say to my soul, Soul, thou hast much
goods laid up for many years; take thine ease, eat, drink,
20 be merry. But God said unto him, Thou foolish one,
this night is thy soul required of thee; and the things
21 which thou hast prepared, whose shall they be? So is he
that layeth up treasure for himself, and is not rich toward
God.

B. Of Watchfulness

Let your loins be girded about, and your lamps 35
burning; and be ye yourselves like unto men looking 36
for their lord, when he shall return from the marriage
feast; that, when he cometh and knocketh, they may
straightway open unto him. Blessed are those servants, 37
whom the lord when he cometh shall find watching:
verily I say unto you, that he shall gird himself, and make
them sit down to meat, and shall come and serve them.
And if he shall come in the second watch, and if in the 38
third, and find them so, blessed are those servants.

And that servant, which knew his lord's will, and made 47
not ready, nor did according to his will, shall be beaten
with many stripes; but he that knew not, and did things 48
worthy of stripes, shall be beaten with few stripes. And
to whomsoever much is given, of him shall much be
required: and to whom they commit much, of him will
they ask the more.

I came to cast fire upon the earth; and what will I, if it 49
is already kindled? But I have a baptism to be baptized 50
with; and how am I straitened till it be accomplished!

C. To Repentance—The Barren Fig Tree

13 Now there were some present at that very season 1
which told him of the Galilæans, whose blood Pilate had
mingled with their sacrifices. And he answered and said 2
unto them, Think ye that these Galilæans were sinners

above all the Galilæans, because they have suffered these
3 things? I tell you, Nay: but, except ye repent, ye shall
4 all in like manner perish.[1] Or those eighteen, upon
whom the tower in Siloam fell, and killed them, think ye
that they were offenders above all the men that dwell in
5 Jerusalem? I tell you, Nay: but, except ye repent, ye
shall all likewise perish.

6   And he spake this parable; A certain man had a fig
tree planted in his vineyard; and he came seeking fruit
7 thereon, and found none. And he said unto the vine-
dresser, Behold, these three years I come seeking fruit
on this fig tree, and find none: cut it down; why doth it
8 also cumber the ground? And he answering saith unto
him, Lord, let it alone this year also, till I shall dig about
9 it, and dung it: and if it bear fruit thenceforth, well; but
if not, thou shalt cut it down.

D. Against Preferring the Letter to the Spirit

10   And he was teaching in one of the synagogues on the
11 sabbath day. And behold, a woman which had a spirit of
infirmity eighteen years; and she was bowed together,
12 and could in no wise lift herself up. And when Jesus saw
her, he called her, and said to her, Woman, thou art
13 loosed from thine infirmity. And he laid his hands upon
her: and immediately she was made straight, and glorified
14 God. And the ruler of the synagogue, being moved with

[1] Cf. p. 25.

indignation because Jesus had healed on the sabbath,[1] answered and said to the multitude, There are six days in which men ought to work: in them therefore come and be healed, and not on the day of the sabbath. But the 15 Lord answered him, and said, Ye hypocrites, doth not each one of you on the sabbath loose his ox or his ass from the stall, and lead him away to watering? And ought not 16 this woman, being a daughter of Abraham, whom Satan had bound, lo, these eighteen years, to have been loosed from this bond on the day of the sabbath? And as he said 17 these things, all his adversaries were put to shame: and all the multitude rejoiced for all the glorious things that were done by him.

E. OF THE PASSION—TO HEROD

In that very hour there came certain Pharisees, saying 31 to him, Get thee out, and go hence: for Herod would fain kill thee. And he said unto them, Go and say to that fox, 32 Behold, I cast out devils and perform cures to-day and to-morrow, and the third day I am perfected. Howbeit 33 I must go on my way to-day and to-morrow and the day following: for it cannot be that a prophet perish out of Jerusalem.

[1] Cf. Mk. iii. 1–6.

F. To Humility and Generosity—The
Great Supper
(cf. Mt. xxii. 1–14 and p. 98)

14 7   And he spake a parable unto those which were bidden, when he marked how they chose out the chief seats; 8 saying unto them, When thou art bidden of any man to a marriage feast, sit not down in the chief seat; lest haply 9 a more honourable man than thou be bidden of him, and he that bade thee and him shall come and say to thee, Give this man place; and then thou shalt begin with 10 shame to take the lowest place. But when thou art bidden, go and sit down in the lowest place; that when he that hath bidden thee cometh, he may say to thee, Friend, go up higher: then shalt thou have glory in the presence of all that sit at meat with thee.

12   And he said to him also that had bidden him, When thou makest a dinner or a supper, call not thy friends, nor thy brethren, nor thy kinsmen, nor rich neighbours; lest haply they also bid thee again, and a recompense be made 13 thee. But when thou makest a feast, bid the poor, the 14 maimed, the lame, the blind: and thou shalt be blessed; because they have not wherewith to recompense thee: for thou shalt be recompensed in the resurrection of the just.

15   And when one of them that sat at meat with him heard these things, he said unto him, Blessed is he that shall eat 16 bread in the kingdom of God. But he said unto him, A certain man made a great supper; and he bade many:

and he sent forth his servant at supper time to say to them 17
that were bidden, Come; for all things are now ready.
And they all with one consent began to make excuse. The 18
first said unto him, I have bought a field, and I must
needs go out and see it: I pray thee have me excused.
And another said, I have bought five yoke of oxen, and 19
I go to prove them: I pray thee have me excused. And 20
another said, I have married a wife, and therefore I cannot
come. And the servant came, and told his lord these 21
things. Then the master of the house being angry said to
his servant, Go out quickly into the streets and lanes of
the city, and bring in hither the poor and maimed and
blind and lame. And the servant said, Lord, what thou 22
didst command is done, and yet there is room. And the 23
lord said unto the servant, Go out into the highways and
hedges, and constrain them to come in, that my house
may be filled. For I say unto you, that none of those men 24
which were bidden shall taste of my supper.

G. On Counting the Cost

For which of you, desiring to build a tower, doth not 28
first sit down and count the cost, whether he have wherewith to complete it? Lest haply, when he hath laid a 29
foundation, and is not able to finish, all that behold begin
to mock him, saying, This man began to build, and was 30
not able to finish. Or what king, as he goeth to encounter 31
another king in war, will not sit down first and take
counsel whether he is able with ten thousand to meet him
that cometh against him with twenty thousand? Or else, 32

while the other is yet a great way off, he sendeth an
33 ambassage, and asketh conditions of peace. So therefore
whosoever he be of you that renounceth not all that he
hath, he cannot be my disciple.

VII. PARABLES OF FORGIVENESS
(cf. pp. 89–90)

A. The Lost Sheep

15 1 Now all the publicans and sinners were drawing near
2 unto him for to hear him. And both the Pharisees and
the scribes murmured, saying, This man receiveth
sinners, and eateth with them.
3, 4   [1]And he spake unto them this parable, saying, What
man of you, having a hundred sheep, and having lost one
of them, doth not leave the ninety and nine in the wilder-
5 ness, and go after that which is lost, until he find it? And
when he hath found it, he layeth it on his shoulders,
6 rejoicing. And when he cometh home, he calleth together
his friends and his neighbours, saying unto them, Rejoice
with me, for I have found my sheep which was lost.
7 I say unto you, that even so there shall be joy in heaven
over one sinner that repenteth, more than over ninety
and nine righteous persons, which need no repentance.

[1] Cf. Mt. xviii. 12, 13. This may therefore belong to Q, though
the application in Mt. is different.

B. The Lost Coin

Or what woman having ten pieces of silver,[1] if she lose 8
one piece, doth not light a lamp, and sweep the house,
and seek diligently until she find it? And when she hath 9
found it, she calleth together her friends and neighbours,
saying, Rejoice with me, for I have found the piece which
I had lost. Even so, I say unto you, there is joy in the 10
presence of the angels of God over one sinner that
repenteth.

C. The Lost Son

And he said, A certain man had two sons: and the 11, 12
younger of them said to his father, Father, give me the
portion of thy substance that falleth to me. And he
divided unto them his living. And not many days after 13
the younger son gathered all together, and took his
journey into a far country; and there he wasted his substance with riotous living. And when he had spent all, 14
there arose a mighty famine in that country; and he began
to be in want. And he went and joined himself to one of 15
the citizens of that country; and he sent him into his
fields to feed swine. And he would fain have been filled 16
with the husks that the swine did eat: and no man gave
unto him. But when he came to himself he said, How 17
many hired servants of my father's have bread enough
and to spare, and I perish here with hunger! I will arise 18
and go to my father, and will say unto him, Father, I have

[1] I.e. drachmæ, Greek coins equal in value to the denarius, or
to a quarter of the Jewish shekel.

19 sinned against heaven, and in thy sight: I am no more worthy to be called thy son: make me as one of thy hired
20 servants. And he arose, and came to his father. But while he was yet afar off, his father saw him, and was moved with compassion, and ran, and fell on his neck,
21 and kissed him. And the son said unto him, Father, I have sinned against heaven, and in thy sight: I am no more
22 worthy to be called thy son. But the father said to his servants, Bring forth quickly the best robe, and put it on him; and put a ring on his hand, and shoes on his feet:
23 and bring the fatted calf, and kill it, and let us eat, and
24 make merry: for this my son was dead, and is alive again; he was lost, and is found. And they began to be merry.
25 Now his elder son was in the field: and as he came and drew nigh to the house, he heard music and dancing.
26 And he called to him one of the servants, and inquired
27 what these things might be. And he said unto him, Thy brother is come; and thy father hath killed the fatted calf,
28 because he hath received him safe and sound. But he was angry, and would not go in: and his father came out,
29 and intreated him. But he answered and said to his father, Lo, these many years do I serve thee, and I never transgressed a commandment of thine: and yet thou never gavest me a kid, that I might make merry with my
30 friends: but when this thy son came, which hath devoured thy living with harlots, thou killedst for him the fatted
31 calf. And he said unto him, Son, thou art ever with me,
32 and all that is mine is thine. But it was meet to make merry and be glad: for this thy brother was dead, and is alive again; and was lost, and is found.

VIII. PARABLES OF RESPONSIBILITY
(cf. pp. 90–1)

A. For the Use of Foresight—The Unjust Steward

16 And he said also unto the disciples, There was a certain 1
rich man, which had a steward; and the same was accused
unto him that he was wasting his goods. And he called 2
him, and said unto him, What is this that I hear of thee?
render the account of thy stewardship; for thou canst be
no longer steward. And the steward said within himself, 3
What shall I do, seeing that my lord taketh away the
stewardship from me? I have not strength to dig; to beg
I am ashamed. I am resolved what to do, that, when I am 4
put out of the stewardship, they may receive me into their
houses. And calling to him each one of his lord's debtors, 5
he said to the first, How much owest thou unto my lord?
And he said, A hundred measures of oil. And he said 6
unto him, Take thy bond, and sit down quickly and
write fifty. Then said he to another, And how much 7
owest thou? And he said, A hundred measures of wheat.
He saith unto him, Take thy bond, and write fourscore.
And his lord commended the unrighteous steward 8
because he had done wisely:[1] for the sons of this world
are for their own generation wiser than the sons of the
light. And I say unto you, Make to yourselves friends by 9
means of the mammon of unrighteousness; that, when
it shall fail, they may receive you into the eternal tabernacles. He that is faithful in a very little is faithful also 10

[1] "Shrewdly" or "with foresight".

in much: and he that is unrighteous in a very little is
11 unrighteous also in much. If therefore ye have not been
faithful in the unrighteous mammon, who will commit
12 to your trust the true riches? And if ye have not been
faithful in that which is another's, who will give you that
which is your own?

B. For the Use of Money—Dives and Lazarus

14 And the Pharisees, who were lovers of money, heard
15 all these things; and they scoffed at him. And he said
unto them, Ye are they that justify yourselves in the sight
of men; but God knoweth your hearts: for that which is
exalted among men is an abomination in the sight of God.
19 Now there was a certain rich man, and he was clothed
in purple and fine linen, faring sumptuously every day:
20 and a certain beggar named Lazarus was laid at his gate,
21 full of sores, and desiring to be fed with the crumbs that
fell from the rich man's table; yea, even the dogs came
22 and licked his sores. And it came to pass, that the beggar
died, and that he was carried away by the angels into
Abraham's bosom:[1] and the rich man also died, and was
23 buried. And in Hades[2] he lifted up his eyes, being in
torments, and seeth Abraham afar off, and Lazarus in
24 his bosom. And he cried and said, Father Abraham,
have mercy on me, and send Lazarus, that he may dip

[1] I.e. in the place next to Abraham at the heavenly feast; cf. Jn. xiv. 23 and xxi. 20.
[2] Here apparently identical with Gehenna, as the place of torment.

the tip of his finger in water, and cool my tongue; for I am in anguish in this flame. But Abraham said, Son, 25 remember that thou in thy lifetime receivedst thy good things, and Lazarus in like manner evil things: but now here he is comforted, and thou art in anguish. And 26 beside all this, between us and you there is a great gulf fixed, that they which would pass from hence to you may not be able, and that none may cross over from thence to us. And he said, I pray thee therefore, father, that thou 27 wouldest send him to my father's house; for I have five 28 brethren; that he may testify unto them, lest they also come into this place of torment. But Abraham saith, 29 They have Moses and the prophets; let them hear them. And he said, Nay, father Abraham: but if one go to them 30 from the dead, they will repent. And he said unto him, 31 If they hear not Moses and the prophets, neither will they be persuaded, if one rise from the dead.

C. FOR THE USE OF GRATITUDE—AN ACT
OF MERCY
(cf. ix. 51 ff.)

17   And it came to pass, as they were on the way to Jeru- 11 salem, that he was passing through the midst of Samaria and Galilee.[1] And as he entered into a certain village, 12 there met him ten men that were lepers, which stood afar off: and they lifted up their voices, saying, Jesus, Master, 13 have mercy on us. And when he saw them, he said unto 14 them, Go and shew yourselves unto the priests. And it

---

[1] I.e. along the boundary between them.

15 came to pass, as they went, they were cleansed. And one
of them, when he saw that he was healed, turned back,
16 with a loud voice glorifying God; and he fell upon his
face at his feet, giving him thanks: and he was a Samari-
17 tan. And Jesus answering said, Were not the ten cleansed?
18 but where are the nine? Were there none found that
19 returned to give glory to God, save this stranger? And
he said unto him, Arise, and go thy way: thy faith hath
made thee whole.

20 And being asked by the Pharisees, when the kingdom
of God cometh, he answered them and said, The king-
21 dom of God cometh not with observation: neither shall
they say, Lo, here! or, There! for lo, the kingdom of God
is within you.

D. For the Use of Persistence—The Unjust Judge

(cf. xi. 5–8 and p. 94)

18 1 And he spake a parable unto them to the end that they
2 ought always to pray, and not to faint; saying, There was
in a city a judge, which feared not God, and regarded not
3 man: and there was a widow in that city; and she came
oft unto him, saying, Avenge[1] me of mine adversary.
4 And he would not for a while: but afterward he said
within himself, Though I fear not God, nor regard man;
5 yet because this widow troubleth me, I will avenge her,
6 lest she wear me out by her continual coming. And the
7 Lord said, Hear what the unrighteous judge saith. And

[1] I.e. vindicate.

shall not God avenge his elect, which cry to him day and night, and he is longsuffering over them? I say unto you, 8 that he will avenge them speedily. Howbeit when the Son of man cometh, shall he find faith on the earth?

E. For the Use of Prayer—The Pharisee and the Publican
(cf. p. 94)

And he spake also this parable unto certain which 9 trusted in themselves that they were righteous, and set all others at nought: Two men went up into the temple 10 to pray; the one a Pharisee, and the other a publican. The Pharisee stood and prayed thus with himself, God, 11 I thank thee, that I am not as the rest of men, extortioners, unjust, adulterers, or even as this publican. I fast twice in the week; I give tithes of all that I get. But 12, 13 the publican, standing afar off, would not lift up so much as his eyes unto heaven, but smote his breast, saying, God, be merciful to me a sinner. I say unto you, This 14 man went down to his house justified rather than the other: for every one that exalteth himself shall be humbled; but he that humbleth himself shall be exalted.

F. For the Use of Opportunities—The Pounds
(cf. Mt. xxv. 14–30 and pp. 98–9)

19 And he entered and was passing through Jericho. And 1, 2 behold, a man called by name Zacchæus; and he was a chief publican, and he was rich. And he sought to see 3

Jesus who he was; and could not for the crowd, because
4 he was little of stature. And he ran on before, and climbed
up into a sycomore tree[1] to see him: for he was to pass
5 that way. And when Jesus came to the place, he looked
up, and said unto him, Zacchæus, make haste, and come
6 down; for to-day I must abide at thy house. And he made
7 haste, and came down, and received him joyfully. And
when they saw it, they all murmured, saying, He is gone
8 in to lodge with a man that is a sinner.[2] And Zacchæus
stood, and said unto the Lord, Behold, Lord, the half of
my goods I give[3] to the poor; and if I have wrongfully
9 exacted aught of any man, I restore fourfold. And Jesus
said unto him, To-day is salvation come to this house,
10 forasmuch as he also is a son of Abraham. For the Son of
man came to seek and to save that which was lost.

11   And as they heard these things, he added and spake
a parable, because he was nigh to Jerusalem, and because
they supposed that the kingdom of God was imme-
12 diately to appear. He said therefore, A certain nobleman[4]
went into a far country, to receive for himself a kingdom,
13 and to return. And he called ten servants of his, and gave
them ten pounds,[5] and said unto them, Trade ye herewith
14 till I come. But his citizens hated him, and sent an
ambassage after him, saying, We will not that this man
15 reign over us. And it came to pass, when he was come
back again, having received the kingdom, that he com-

---

[1] Not our sycamore, but the Egyptian fig.
[2] I.e. outcaste, because a tax-collector.
[3] I.e. now as an act of penitence.
[4] The allusion is probably to Archelaus, son of Herod the Great,
who went to Rome in 4 B.C. to secure his kingdom.
[5] I.e. mina, worth about £4.

manded these servants, unto whom he had given the money, to be called to him, that he might know what they had gained by trading. And the first came before him, 16 saying, Lord, thy pound hath made ten pounds more. And he said unto him, Well done, thou good servant: 17 because thou wast found faithful in a very little, have thou authority over ten cities. And the second came, 18 saying, Thy pound, Lord, hath made five pounds. And 19 he said unto him also, Be thou also over five cities. And 20 another came, saying, Lord, behold, here is thy pound, which I kept laid up in a napkin: for I feared thee, 21 because thou art an austere man: thou takest up that thou layedst not down, and reapest that thou didst not sow. He saith unto him, Out of thine own mouth will 22 I judge thee, thou wicked servant. Thou knewest that I am an austere man, taking up that I laid not down, and reaping that I did not sow; then wherefore gavest thou 23 not my money into the bank, and I at my coming should have required it with interest? And he said unto them 24 that stood by, Take away from him the pound, and give it unto him that hath the ten pounds. And they said unto 25 him, Lord, he hath ten pounds. I say unto you, that 26 unto every one that hath shall be given; but from him that hath not, even that which he hath shall be taken away from him. Howbeit these mine enemies, which 27 would not that I should reign over them, bring hither, and slay them before me.

IX. THE PREPARATION FOR THE PASSION
(cf. Mk. xi. i–xiv. 25)

37   And as he was now drawing nigh, even at the descent of the mount of Olives, the whole multitude of the disciples began to rejoice and praise God with a loud voice for all the mighty works which they had seen;
38 saying, Blessed is the King that cometh in the name of
39 the Lord: peace in heaven, and glory in the highest. And some of the Pharisees from the multitude said unto him,
40 Master, rebuke thy disciples. And he answered and said, I tell you that, if these shall hold their peace, the stones will cry out.

41   And when he drew nigh, he saw the city and wept
42 over it, saying, If thou hadst known in this day, even thou, the things which belong unto peace! but now they
43 are hid from thine eyes. For the days shall come upon thee, when thine enemies shall cast up a bank about thee, and compass thee round, and keep thee in on every side,
44 and shall dash thee to the ground, and thy children within thee; and they shall not leave in thee one stone upon another; because thou knewest not the time of thy visitation.

22 14 And when the hour was come, he sat down, and the
15 apostles with him. And he said unto them, With desire I have desired to eat this passover with you before I
16 suffer: for I say unto you, I will not eat it, until it be
17 fulfilled in the kingdom of God. And he received a cup, and when he had given thanks, he said, Take this, and
18 divide it among yourselves: for I say unto you, I will not

drink from henceforth of the fruit of the vine, until the kingdom of God shall come. *And he took bread, and 19 when he had given thanks, he brake it, and gave to them, saying, This is my body which is given for you: this do in remembrance of me. And the cup in like manner after 20 supper, saying, This cup is the new covenant in my blood, even that which is poured out for you.* But behold, the 21 hand of him that betrayeth me is with me on the table. For the Son of man indeed goeth, as it hath been deter- 22 mined: but woe unto that man through whom he is betrayed! And they began to question among them- 23 selves, which of them it was that should do this thing[1].

And he said unto them, Simon, Simon, behold, Satan 31 asked to have you, that he might sift you as wheat: but 32 I made supplication for thee, that thy faith fail not: and do thou, when once thou hast turned again, stablish thy brethren. And he said unto him, Lord, with thee I am 33 ready to go both to prison and to death. And he said, 34 I tell thee, Peter, the cock shall not crow this day, until thou shalt thrice deny that thou knowest me.

And he said unto them, When I sent you forth without 35 purse, and wallet, and shoes, lacked ye anything? And they said, Nothing. And he said unto them, But now, 36 he that hath a purse, let him take it, and likewise a wallet: and he that hath none, let him sell his cloke, and buy a sword. For I say unto you, that this which is 37 written must be fulfilled in me, And he was reckoned

* This passage and several others similarly marked in chapter xxiv are omitted in Codex D and other Western texts: they are probably later insertions—in this passage from 1 Cor. xi. 24-5.
[1] For vv. 24-7 cf. Mk. x. 41-5; for vv. 28-30 Mt. xix. 28.

with transgressors: for that which concerneth me hath
38 fulfilment. And they said, Lord, behold, here are two
swords. And he said unto them, It is enough.

X. THE CRUCIFIXION AND
RESURRECTION
(cf. Mk. xiv. 26 to end and pp. 76–8)

39   And he came out, and went, as his custom was, unto
the mount of Olives; and the disciples also followed him.
40 And when he was at the place, he said unto them, Pray
41 that ye enter not into temptation. And he was parted
from them about a stone's cast; and he kneeled down and
42 prayed, saying, Father, if thou be willing, remove this
cup from me: nevertheless not my will, but thine, be
43 done. †And there appeared unto him an angel from
44 heaven, strengthening him. And being in an agony he
prayed more earnestly: and his sweat became as it were
great drops of blood falling down upon the ground.†
45 And when he rose up from his prayer, he came unto the
46 disciples, and found them sleeping for sorrow, and said
unto them, Why sleep ye? rise and pray, that ye enter
not into temptation.

47   While he yet spake, behold, a multitude, and he that
was called Judas, one of the twelve, went before them;
48 and he drew near unto Jesus to kiss him. But Jesus said
unto him, Judas, betrayest thou the Son of man with a
49 kiss? And when they that were about him saw what
would follow, they said, Lord, shall we smite with the
50 sword? And a certain one of them smote the servant of
51 the high priest, and struck off his right ear. But Jesus

† The best MSS. omit these verses.

answered and said, Suffer ye thus far. And he touched his ear, and healed him. And Jesus said unto the chief 52 priests, and captains of the temple, and elders, which were come against him, Are ye come out, as against a robber, with swords and staves? When I was daily with 53 you in the temple, ye stretched not forth your hands against me: but this is your hour, and the power of darkness.

And they seized him, and led him away, and brought 54 him into the high priest's house. But Peter followed afar off. And when they had kindled a fire in the midst of the 55 court, and had sat down together, Peter sat in the midst of them. And a certain maid seeing him as he sat in the 56 light of the fire, and looking stedfastly upon him, said, This man also was with him. But he denied, saying, 57 Woman, I know him not. And after a little while another 58 saw him, and said, Thou also art one of them. But Peter said, Man, I am not. And after the space of about one 59 hour another confidently affirmed, saying, Of a truth this man also was with him: for he is a Galilæan. But 60 Peter said, Man, I know not what thou sayest. And immediately, while he yet spake, the cock crew. And the 61 Lord turned, and looked upon Peter. And Peter remembered the word of the Lord, how that he said unto him, Before the cock crow this day, thou shalt deny me thrice. And he went out, and wept bitterly. 62

And the men that held Jesus mocked him, and beat 63 him. And they blindfolded him, and asked him, saying, 64 Prophesy: who is he that struck thee? And many other 65 things spake they against him, reviling him.

And as soon as it was day, the assembly of the elders 66

of the people was gathered together, both chief priests
and scribes; and they led him away into their council,
67 saying, If thou art the Christ, tell us. But he said unto
68 them, If I tell you, ye will not believe: and if I ask you,
69 ye will not answer. But from henceforth shall the Son of
man be seated at the right hand of the power of God.
70 And they all said, Art thou then the Son of God? And
71 he said unto them, Ye say that I am. And they said,
What further need have we of witness? for we ourselves
have heard from his own mouth.

23 1 And the whole company of them rose up, and brought
2 him before Pilate. And they began to accuse him, saying,
We found this man perverting our nation, and forbidding
to give tribute to Cæsar, and saying that he himself is
3 Christ a king. And Pilate asked him, saying, Art thou
the King of the Jews? And he answered him and said,
4 Thou sayest. And Pilate said unto the chief priests and
5 the multitudes, I find no fault in this man. But they
were the more urgent, saying, He stirreth up the people,
teaching throughout all Judæa, and beginning from
6 Galilee even unto this place. But when Pilate heard it,
7 he asked whether the man were a Galilæan. And when
he knew that he was of Herod's jurisdiction, he sent him
unto Herod, who himself also was at Jerusalem in these
days.

8 Now when Herod saw Jesus, he was exceeding glad:
for he was of a long time desirous to see him, because he
had heard concerning him; and he hoped to see some
9 miracle done by him. And he questioned him in many
10 words; but he answered him nothing. And the chief
priests and the scribes stood, vehemently accusing him.

And Herod with his soldiers set him at nought, and 11 mocked him, and arraying him in gorgeous apparel sent him back to Pilate. And Herod and Pilate became friends 12 with each other that very day: for before they were at enmity between themselves.

And Pilate called together the chief priests and the 13 rulers and the people, and said unto them, Ye brought 14 unto me this man, as one that perverteth the people: and behold, I, having examined him before you, found no fault in this man touching those things whereof ye accuse him: no, nor yet Herod: for he sent him back unto us; 15 and behold, nothing worthy of death hath been done by him. I will therefore chastise him, and release him. But 16, 18 they cried out all together, saying, Away with this man, and release unto us Barabbas: one who for a certain 19 insurrection made in the city, and for murder, was cast into prison. And Pilate spake unto them again, desiring 20 to release Jesus; but they shouted, saying, Crucify, 21 crucify him. And he said unto them the third time, Why, 22 what evil hath this man done? I have found no cause of death in him: I will therefore chastise him and release him. But they were instant with loud voices, asking that 23 he might be crucified. And their voices prevailed. And 24 Pilate gave sentence that what they asked for should be done. And he released him that for insurrection and 25 murder had been cast into prison, whom they asked for; but Jesus he delivered up to their will.

And when they led him away, they laid hold upon one 26 Simon of Cyrene, coming from the country, and laid on him the cross, to bear it after Jesus.

And there followed him a great multitude of the people, 27

28 and of women who bewailed and lamented him. But Jesus turning unto them said, Daughters of Jerusalem, weep not for me, but weep for yourselves, and for your

29 children. For behold, the days are coming, in which they shall say, Blessed are the barren, and the wombs that

30 never bare, and the breasts that never gave suck. Then shall they begin to say to the mountains, Fall on us; and

31 to the hills, Cover us. For if they do these things in the green tree, what shall be done in the dry?[1]

32 And there were also two others, malefactors, led with him to be put to death.

33 And when they came unto the place which is called The skull, there they crucified him, and the malefactors,

34 one on the right hand and the other on the left. And Jesus said, Father, forgive them; for they know not what they do. And parting his garments among them, they

35 cast lots. And the people stood beholding. And the rulers also scoffed at him, saying, He saved others; let him save himself, if this is the Christ of God, his chosen.

36 And the soldiers also mocked him, coming to him,

37 offering him vinegar, and saying, If thou art the King of

38 the Jews, save thyself. And there was also a superscription over him, THIS IS THE KING OF THE JEWS.

39 And one of the malefactors which were hanged railed on him, saying, Art not thou the Christ? save thyself and

40 us. But the other answered, and rebuking him said, Dost thou not even fear God, seeing thou art in the same con-

41 demnation? And we indeed justly; for we receive the due reward of our deeds: but this man hath done nothing

---

[1] An allusion like the Barren Fig Tree (xiii. 6–9) to the Jewish nation.

amiss. And he said, Jesus, remember me when thou 42
comest in thy kingdom. And he said unto him, Verily 43
I say unto thee, To-day shalt thou be with me in Paradise.

And it was now about the sixth hour, and a darkness 44
came over the whole land until the ninth hour, the sun's 45
light failing: and the veil of the temple was rent in the
midst. And when Jesus had cried with a loud voice, he 46
said, Father, into thy hands I commend my spirit: and
having said this, he gave up the ghost. And when the 47
centurion saw what was done, he glorified God, saying,
Certainly this was a righteous man. And all the multi- 48
tudes that came together to this sight, when they beheld
the things that were done, returned smiting their breasts.
And all his acquaintance, and the women that followed 49
with him from Galilee, stood afar off, seeing these
things.

And behold, a man named Joseph, who was a coun- 50
cillor, a good man and a righteous (he had not consented 51
to their counsel and deed), a man of Arimathæa, a city
of the Jews, who was looking for the kingdom of God:
this man went to Pilate, and asked for the body of Jesus. 52
And he took it down, and wrapped it in a linen cloth, 53
and laid him in a tomb that was hewn in stone, where
never man had yet lain. And it was the day of the Pre- 54
paration, and the sabbath drew on. And the women, 55
which had come with him out of Galilee, followed after,
and beheld the tomb, and how his body was laid. And 56
they returned, and prepared spices and ointments.

And on the sabbath they rested according to the com-
24 mandment. But on the first day of the week, at early 1
dawn, they came unto the tomb, bringing the spices

2 which they had prepared. And they found the stone
3 rolled away from the tomb. And they entered in, and
4 found not the body *of the Lord Jesus.* And it came to
pass, while they were perplexed thereabout, behold, two
5 men stood by them in dazzling apparel: and as they were
affrighted, and bowed down their faces to the earth, they
said unto them, Why seek ye the living among the dead?
6 *He is not here, but is risen:* remember how he spake
7 unto you when he was yet in Galilee,[1] saying that the
Son of man must be delivered up into the hands of sinful
8 men, and be crucified, and the third day rise again. And
9 they remembered his words, and returned from the
tomb, and told all these things to the eleven, and to all
10 the rest. Now they were Mary Magdalene, and Joanna,[2]
and Mary the mother of James: and the other women
11 with them told these things unto the apostles. And these
words appeared in their sight as idle talk; and they
12 disbelieved them. *But Peter arose, and ran unto the
tomb; and stooping and looking in, he seeth the linen
cloths by themselves; and he departed to his home,
wondering at that which was come to pass.*
13   And behold, two of them were going that very day to
a village named Emmaus, which was threescore furlongs
14 from Jerusalem. And they communed with each other
15 of all these things which had happened. And it came to
pass, while they communed and questioned together,
16 that Jesus himself drew near, and went with them. But
their eyes were holden that they should not know him.

---

* Cf. xxii. 19, note.
[1] This Gospel contains no reference to appearances in Galilee;
cf. Mk. xvi. 7 and p. 77.   [2] Cf. viii. 3.

And he said unto them, What communications are these 17
that ye have one with another, as ye walk? And they
stood still, looking sad. And one of them, named Cleopas, 18
answering said unto him, Dost thou alone sojourn in
Jerusalem and not know the things which are come to
pass there in these days? And he said unto them, What 19
things? And they said unto him, The things concerning
Jesus of Nazareth, which was a prophet mighty in deed
and word before God and all the people: and how the 20
chief priests and our rulers delivered him up to be condemned to death, and crucified him. But we hoped that 21
it was he which should redeem Israel. Yea and beside all
this, it is now the third day since these things came to
pass. Moreover certain women of our company amazed 22
us, having been early at the tomb; and when they found 23
not his body, they came, saying, that they had also seen
a vision of angels, which said that he was alive. And 24
certain of them that were with us went to the tomb, and
found it even so as the women had said: but him they
saw not. And he said unto them, O foolish men, and 25
slow of heart to believe in all that the prophets have
spoken! Behoved it not the Christ to suffer these things, 26
and to enter into his glory? And beginning from Moses 27
and from all the prophets, he interpreted to them in all
the scriptures the things concerning himself. And they 28
drew nigh unto the village, whither they were going:
and he made as though he would go further. And they 29
constrained him, saying, Abide with us: for it is toward
evening, and the day is now far spent. And he went in
to abide with them. And it came to pass, when he had 30
sat down with them to meat, he took the bread, and

31 blessed it, and brake, and gave to them. And their eyes were opened, and they knew him; and he vanished out
32 of their sight. And they said one to another, Was not our heart burning within us, while he spake to us in the way, while he opened to us the scriptures?
33 And they rose up that very hour, and returned to Jerusalem, and found the eleven gathered together, and them that were with them,
34 saying, The Lord is risen indeed, and hath appeared to
35 Simon.[1] And they rehearsed the things that happened in the way, and how he was known of them in the breaking of the bread.

36   And as they spake these things, he himself stood in the midst of them, *and saith unto them, Peace be unto
37 you.* But they were terrified and affrighted, and sup-
38 posed that they beheld a spirit. And he said unto them, Why are ye troubled? and wherefore do reasonings arise
39 in your heart? See my hands and my feet, that it is I myself: handle me, and see; for a spirit hath not flesh
40 and bones, as ye behold me having. *And when he had
41 said this, he shewed them his hands and his feet.* And while they still disbelieved for joy, and wondered, he
42 said unto them, Have ye here anything to eat? And they
43 gave him a piece of a broiled fish. And he took it, and did eat before them.

44   And he said unto them, These are my words which I spake unto you, while I was yet with you, how that all things must needs be fulfilled, which are written in the law of Moses, and the prophets, and the psalms, con-
45 cerning me. Then opened he their mind, that they might
46 understand the scriptures; and he said unto them, Thus

[1] St Paul mentions this appearance in 1 Cor. xv. 5.

it is written, that the Christ should suffer, and rise again
from the dead the third day; and that repentance and   47
remission of sins should be preached in his name unto all
the nations, beginning from Jerusalem. Ye are witnesses   48
of these things. And behold, I send forth the promise   49
of my Father upon you: but tarry ye in the city, until ye
be clothed with power from on high.

And he led them out until they were over against   50
Bethany: and he lifted up his hands, and blessed them.
And it came to pass, while he blessed them, he parted   51
from them, *and was carried up into heaven.* And they   52
worshipped him, and returned to Jerusalem with great
joy: and were continually in the temple, blessing God.   53

Teaching and Parables contained only in the Gospel according to St Matthew

I. THE SERMON ON THE MOUNT
(for much of this cf. Q, especially pp. 165–8)

5 And seeing the multitudes, Jesus went up into the moun- 1
tain: and when he had sat down, his disciples came unto
him: and he opened his mouth and taught them, saying, 2
[1]Blessed are the poor in spirit: for theirs is the kingdom 3
of heaven.

Blessed are they that mourn: for they shall be com- 4
forted.

Blessed are the meek: for they shall inherit the earth. 5

Blessed are they that hunger and thirst after righteous- 6
ness: for they shall be filled.

Blessed are the merciful: for they shall obtain mercy. 7

Blessed are the pure in heart: for they shall see God. 8

Blessed are the peacemakers: for they shall be called 9
sons of God.

Blessed are they that have been persecuted for 10
righteousness' sake: for theirs is the kingdom of heaven.
Blessed are ye when men shall reproach you, and per- 11
secute you, and say all manner of evil against you falsely,
for my sake. Rejoice, and be exceeding glad: for great 12
is your reward in heaven: for so persecuted they the
prophets which were before you.

[1] For the Beatitudes cf. Q (Lk. vi. 20–3).

14 Ye are the light of the world. A city set on a hill cannot
15 be hid. Neither do men light a lamp, and put it under the
bushel, but on the stand; and it shineth unto all that are
16 in the house. Even so let your light shine before men,
that they may see your good works, and glorify your
Father which is in heaven.

17 Think not that I came to destroy the law or the
prophets: I came not to destroy, but to fulfil.

19 Whosoever therefore shall break one of these least
commandments, and shall teach men so, shall be called
least in the kingdom of heaven: but whosoever shall do
and teach them, he shall be called great in the kingdom of
20 heaven. For I say unto you, that except your righteousness shall exceed the righteousness of the scribes and
Pharisees, ye shall in no wise enter into the kingdom of
heaven.

21 Ye have heard that it was said to them of old time,
Thou shalt not kill; and whosoever shall kill shall be in
22 danger of the judgement: but I say unto you, that every
one who is angry with his brother shall be in danger of
the judgement; and whosoever shall say to his brother,
Raca, shall be in danger of the council; and whosoever
shall say, Thou fool, shall be in danger of the hell of fire.
23 If therefore thou art offering thy gift at the altar, and
there rememberest that thy brother hath aught against
24 thee, leave there thy gift before the altar, and go thy way,
first be reconciled to thy brother, and then come and
offer thy gift.

27 Ye have heard that it was said, Thou shalt not commit
28 adultery: but I say unto you, that every one that looketh
on a woman to lust after her hath committed adultery

with her already in his heart. And if thy right eye causeth 29
thee to stumble, pluck it out, and cast it from thee: for it
is profitable for thee that one of thy members should
perish, and not thy whole body be cast into hell. And if 30
thy right hand causeth thee to stumble, cut it off, and
cast it from thee: for it is profitable for thee that one of
thy members should perish, and not thy whole body go
into hell.

Again, ye have heard that it was said to them of old 33
time, Thou shalt not forswear thyself, but shalt perform
unto the Lord thine oaths: but I say unto you, Swear not 34
at all; neither by the heaven, for it is the throne of God;
nor by the earth, for it is the footstool of his feet; nor by 35
Jerusalem, for it is the city of the great King. Neither 36
shalt thou swear by thy head, for thou canst not make one
hair white or black. But let your speech be, Yea, yea; 37
Nay, nay: and whatsoever is more than these is of the
evil one.

Ye have heard that it was said, An eye for an eye, and 38
a tooth for a tooth: but I say unto you, Resist not him 39
that is evil.

And whosoever shall compel thee to go one mile, go 41
with him twain.

Ye have heard that it was said, Thou shalt love thy 43
neighbour, and hate thine enemy: but I say unto you,[1] 44
Love your enemies, and pray for them that persecute
you; that ye may be sons of your Father which is in 45
heaven: for he maketh his sun to rise on the evil and the
good, and sendeth rain on the just and the unjust.

6 Take heed that ye do not your righteousness before 1

[1] Cf. Q, p. 166 (Lk. vi. 27–8).

men, to be seen of them: else ye have no reward with your Father which is in heaven.

2 When therefore thou doest alms, sound not a trumpet before thee, as the hypocrites do in the synagogues and in the streets, that they may have glory of men. Verily I say unto you, They have received their reward.

5 And when ye pray, ye shall not be as the hypocrites: for they love to stand and pray in the synagogues and in the corners of the streets, that they may be seen of men. Verily I say unto you, They have received their reward.

6 But thou, when thou prayest, enter into thine inner chamber, and having shut thy door, pray to thy Father which is in secret, and thy Father which seeth in secret

7 shall recompense thee. And in praying use not vain repetitions, as the Gentiles do: for they think that they

8 shall be heard for their much speaking. Be not therefore like unto them: for your Father knoweth what things ye have need of, before ye ask him.

14 For if ye forgive men their trespasses, your heavenly

15 Father will also forgive you. But if ye forgive not men their trespasses, neither will your Father forgive your trespasses.

16 Moreover when ye fast, be not, as the hypocrites, of a sad countenance: for they disfigure their faces, that they may be seen of men to fast. Verily I say unto you,

17 They have received their reward. But thou, when thou

18 fastest, anoint thy head, and wash thy face; that thou be not seen of men to fast, but of thy Father which is in secret: and thy Father, which seeth in secret, shall recompense thee.

34 Be not therefore anxious for the morrow: for the

morrow will be anxious for itself. Sufficient unto the day is the evil thereof.

7 Give not that which is holy unto the dogs, neither cast 6 your pearls before the swine, lest haply they trample them under their feet, and turn and rend you.

Beware of false prophets, which come to you in sheep's 15 clothing, but inwardly are ravening wolves.

II. PARABLES OF THE KINGDOM
(cf. pp. 88–9)

13 Another parable set he before them, saying, The 24 kingdom of heaven is likened unto a man that sowed good seed in his field: but while men slept, his enemy came 25 and sowed tares also among the wheat, and went away. But when the blade sprang up, and brought forth fruit, 26 then appeared the tares also. And the servants of the 27 householder came and said unto him, Sir, didst thou not sow good seed in thy field? whence then hath it tares? And he said unto them, An enemy hath done this. And 28 the servants say unto him, Wilt thou then that we go and gather them up? But he saith, Nay; lest haply while ye 29 gather up the tares, ye root up the wheat with them. Let 30 both grow together until the harvest: and in the time of the harvest I will say to the reapers, Gather up first the tares, and bind them in bundles to burn them: but gather the wheat into my barn.

Then he left the multitudes, and went into the house: 36 and his disciples came unto him, saying, Explain unto us the parable of the tares of the field. And he answered 37

and said, He that soweth the good seed is the Son of man;
38 and the field is the world; and the good seed, these are
the sons of the kingdom; and the tares are the sons of the
39 evil one; and the enemy that sowed them is the devil:
and the harvest is the end of the world; and the reapers
40 are angels. As therefore the tares are gathered up and
burned with fire; so shall it be in the end of the world.
41 The Son of man shall send forth his angels, and they shall
gather out of his kingdom all things that cause stumbling,
42 and them that do iniquity, and shall cast them into the
furnace of fire: there shall be the weeping and gnashing
43 of teeth. Then shall the righteous shine forth as the sun
in the kingdom of their Father. He that hath ears, let
him hear.

44   The kingdom of heaven is like unto a treasure hidden
in the field; which a man found, and hid; and in his joy
he goeth and selleth all that he hath, and buyeth that
field.

45   Again, the kingdom of heaven is like unto a man that
46 is a merchant seeking goodly pearls: and having found
one pearl of great price, he went and sold all that he had,
and bought it.

47   Again, the kingdom of heaven is like unto a net, that
48 was cast into the sea, and gathered of every kind: which,
when it was filled, they drew up on the beach; and they
sat down, and gathered the good into vessels, but the bad
49 they cast away. So shall it be in the end of the world: the
angels shall come forth, and sever the wicked from among
50 the righteous, and shall cast them into the furnace of fire:
there shall be the weeping and gnashing of teeth.

51   Have ye understood all these things? They say unto

him, Yea. And he said unto them, Therefore every scribe 52
who hath been made a disciple to the kingdom of heaven
is like unto a man that is a householder, which bringeth
forth out of his treasure things new and old.

III. PARABLES OF JUDGEMENT
(cf. p. 94)

A. The Two Debtors

18 Then came Peter, and said to him, Lord, how oft shall 21
my brother sin against me, and I forgive him? until seven
times? Jesus saith unto him, I say not unto thee, Until 22
seven times; but, Until seventy times seven. Therefore 23
is the kingdom of heaven likened unto a certain king,
which would make a reckoning with his servants. And 24
when he had begun to reckon, one was brought unto him,
which owed him ten thousand talents. But forasmuch 25
as he had not wherewith to pay, his lord commanded him
to be sold, and his wife, and children, and all that he had,
and payment to be made. The servant therefore fell down 26
and worshipped him, saying, Lord, have patience with
me, and I will pay thee all. And the lord of that servant, 27
being moved with compassion, released him, and forgave
him the debt. But that servant went out, and found one 28
of his fellow-servants, which owed him a hundred pence:
and he laid hold on him, and took him by the throat,
saying, Pay what thou owest. So his fellow-servant fell 29
down and besought him, saying, Have patience with me,
and I will pay thee. And he would not: but went and cast 30

him into prison, till he should pay that which was due.
31 So when his fellow-servants saw what was done, they
were exceeding sorry, and came and told unto their lord
32 all that was done. Then his lord called him unto him, and
saith to him, Thou wicked servant, I forgave thee all that
33 debt, because thou besoughtest me: shouldest not thou
also have had mercy on thy fellow-servant, even as I had
34 mercy on thee? And his lord was wroth, and delivered
him to the tormentors, till he should pay all that was due.
35 So shall also my heavenly Father do unto you, if ye forgive
not every one his brother from your hearts.

B. The Labourers in the Vineyard
(cf. p. 97)

20 1 For the kingdom of heaven is like unto a man that is
a householder, which went out early in the morning to
2 hire labourers into his vineyard. And when he had agreed
with the labourers for a penny a day, he sent them into
3 his vineyard. And he went out about the third hour, and
4 saw others standing in the marketplace idle; and to them
he said, Go ye also into the vineyard, and whatsoever is
5 right I will give you. And they went their way. Again he
went out about the sixth and the ninth hour, and did
6 likewise. And about the eleventh hour he went out, and
found others standing; and he saith unto them, Why
7 stand ye here all the day idle? They say unto him, Because
no man hath hired us. He saith unto them, Go ye also
8 into the vineyard. And when even was come, the lord
of the vineyard saith unto his steward, Call the labourers,

and pay them their hire, beginning from the last unto the first. And when they came that were hired about the eleventh hour, they received every man a penny. And when the first came, they supposed that they would receive more; and they likewise received every man a penny. And when they received it, they murmured against the householder, saying, These last have spent but one hour, and thou hast made them equal unto us, which have borne the burden of the day and the scorching heat. But he answered and said to one of them, Friend, I do thee no wrong: didst not thou agree with me for a penny? Take up that which is thine, and go thy way; it is my will to give unto this last, even as unto thee. Is it not lawful for me to do what I will with mine own? or is thine eye evil, because I am good? So the last shall be first, and the first last.

C. The Two Sons
(cf. pp. 97–8)

21 But what think ye? A man had two sons; and he came to the first, and said, Son, go work to-day in the vineyard. And he answered and said, I will not: but afterward he repented himself, and went. And he came to the second, and said likewise. And he answered and said, I go, sir: and went not. Whether of the twain did the will of his father? They say, The first. Jesus saith unto them, Verily I say unto you, that the publicans and the harlots go into the kingdom of God before you.

D. The Marriage Feast and
Wedding-Garment

(cf. p. 98)

22 1 And Jesus answered and spake again in parables unto
2 them, saying, The kingdom of heaven is likened unto a
certain king, which made a marriage feast for his son,
3 and sent forth his servants to call them that were bidden
4 to the marriage feast: and they would not come. Again
he sent forth other servants, saying, Tell them that are
bidden, Behold, I have made ready my dinner: my oxen
and my fatlings are killed, and all things are ready: come
5 to the marriage feast. But they made light of it, and went
their ways, one to his own farm, another to his merchan-
6 dise: and the rest laid hold on his servants, and entreated
7 them shamefully, and killed them. But the king was
wroth; and he sent his armies, and destroyed those
8 murderers, and burned their city. Then saith he to his
servants, The wedding is ready, but they that were
9 bidden were not worthy. Go ye therefore unto the
partings of the highways, and as many as ye shall find,
10 bid to the marriage feast. And those servants went out
into the highways, and gathered together all as many as
they found, both bad and good: and the wedding was
11 filled with guests. But when the king came in to behold
the guests, he saw there a man which had not on a
12 wedding-garment: and he saith unto him, Friend, how
camest thou in hither not having a wedding-garment?
13 And he was speechless. Then the king said to the servants,
Bind him hand and foot, and cast him out into the outer

darkness; there shall be the weeping and gnashing of
teeth. For many are called, but few chosen.   14

E. The Ten Virgins
(cf. p. 98)

25 Then shall the kingdom of heaven be likened unto ten 1
virgins, which took their lamps, and went forth to meet
the bridegroom. And five of them were foolish, and five 2
were wise. For the foolish, when they took their lamps, 3
took no oil with them: but the wise took oil in their vessels 4
with their lamps. Now while the bridegroom tarried, 5
they all slumbered and slept. But at midnight there is 6
a cry, Behold, the bridegroom! Come ye forth to meet
him. Then all those virgins arose, and trimmed their 7
lamps. And the foolish said unto the wise, Give us of 8
your oil; for our lamps are going out. But the wise 9
answered, saying, Peradventure there will not be enough
for us and you: go ye rather to them that sell, and buy for
yourselves. And while they went away to buy, the bride- 10
groom came; and they that were ready went in with him
to the marriage feast: and the door was shut. Afterward 11
come also the other virgins, saying, Lord, Lord, open
to us. But he answered and said, Verily I say unto you, 12
I know you not. Watch therefore, for ye know not the 13
day nor the hour.

F. The Talents
(cf. pp. 98–9)

For it is as when a man, going into another country, 14
called his own servants, and delivered unto them his

15 goods. And unto one he gave five talents, to another two, to another one; to each according to his several ability;

16 and he went on his journey. Straightway he that received the five talents went and traded with them, and made

17 other five talents. In like manner he also that received

18 the two gained other two. But he that received the one went away and digged in the earth, and hid his lord's

19 money. Now after a long time the lord of those servants

20 cometh, and maketh a reckoning with them. And he that received the five talents came and brought other five talents, saying, Lord, thou deliveredst unto me five

21 talents: lo, I have gained other five talents. His lord said unto him, Well done, good and faithful servant: thou hast been faithful over a few things, I will set thee over

22 many things: enter thou into the joy of thy lord. And he also that received the two talents came and said, Lord, thou deliveredst unto me two talents: lo, I have gained

23 other two talents. His lord said unto him, Well done, good and faithful servant; thou hast been faithful over a few things, I will set thee over many things: enter thou

24 into the joy of thy lord. And he also that had received the one talent came and said, Lord, I knew thee that thou art a hard man, reaping where thou didst not sow, and

25 gathering where thou didst not scatter: and I was afraid, and went away and hid thy talent in the earth: lo, thou

26 hast thine own. But his lord answered and said unto him, Thou wicked and slothful servant, thou knewest that I reap where I sowed not, and gather where I did not

27 scatter; thou oughtest therefore to have put my money to the bankers, and at my coming I should have received

28 back mine own with interest. Take ye away therefore the

talent from him, and give it unto him that hath the ten 29
talents. For unto every one that hath shall be given, and
he shall have abundance: but from him that hath not, 30
even that which he hath shall be taken away. And cast
ye out the unprofitable servant into the outer darkness:
there shall be the weeping and gnashing of teeth.

G. The Sheep and the Goats
(cf. pp. 99, 100)

But when the Son of man shall come in his glory, and 31
all the angels with him, then shall he sit on the throne of
his glory: and before him shall be gathered all the nations: 32
and he shall separate them one from another, as the
shepherd separateth the sheep from the goats: and he 33
shall set the sheep on his right hand, but the goats on the
left. Then shall the King say unto them on his right hand, 34
Come, ye blessed of my Father, inherit the kingdom
prepared for you from the foundation of the world: for 35
I was an hungred, and ye gave me meat: I was thirsty,
and ye gave me drink: I was a stranger, and ye took me
in; naked, and ye clothed me: I was sick, and ye visited 36
me: I was in prison, and ye came unto me. Then shall 37
the righteous answer him, saying, Lord, when saw we
thee an hungred, and fed thee? or athirst, and gave thee
drink? And when saw we thee a stranger, and took thee 38
in? or naked, and clothed thee? And when saw we thee 39
sick, or in prison, and came unto thee? And the King 40
shall answer and say unto them, Verily I say unto you,
Inasmuch as ye did it unto one of these my brethren,

41 even these least, ye did it unto me. Then shall he say also unto them on the left hand, Depart from me, ye cursed, into the eternal fire which is prepared for the devil and 42 his angels: for I was an hungred, and ye gave me no 43 meat: I was thirsty, and ye gave me no drink: I was a stranger, and ye took me not in; naked, and ye clothed 44 me not; sick, and in prison, and ye visited me not. Then shall they also answer, saying, Lord, when saw we thee an hungred, or athirst, or a stranger, or naked, or sick, 45 or in prison, and did not minister unto thee? Then shall he answer them, saying, Verily I say unto you, Inasmuch as ye did it not unto one of these least, ye did it not unto 46 me. And these shall go away into eternal punishment: but the righteous into eternal life.

[Much of the matter peculiar to the First Gospel is concerned with proofs of the fulfilment of Old Testament prophecies, with controversy against the Pharisees, with details concerning St Peter, and with points of apologetic rather than historical importance. These are omitted.]

The problems of the historical value of the Fourth Gospel and of its relation to the other three, first raised in the third century, are not yet solved. Its account of the length and locality of the ministry and of the character of the teaching differs widely from theirs. But no study of the life of our Lord would be complete without reference to it; and for the sake of comparison with the Synoptic record the earlier chapters dealing with events in Galilee are here printed. The sequence of events is not easy to determine and has perhaps been disarranged in one or two places: but it has been indicated in the Introduction (cf. pp. 53–4 and p. 69) how it may stand in relation to the Marcan account. The great discourses which form a large part of its contents and give an unique interpretation of the significance of Christ have been omitted.

For further study reference may be made to—

P. Gardner, *The Ephesian Gospel.*

> C. E. Raven, *Jesus and the Gospel of Love,* chs. vii and viii.

E. F. Scott, *The Fourth Gospel, its Purpose and Theology.*

> R. H. Strachan, *The Fourth Gospel.*

Events of the Ministry in the Gospel according to St John

I. THE WITNESS OF THE BAPTIST

1 And this is the record of John, when the Jews sent 19
priests and Levites from Jerusalem to ask him, Who art
thou? And he confessed, and denied not; but confessed, 20
I am not the Christ. And they asked him, What then? 21
Art thou Elias? And he saith, I am not.[1] Art thou that
prophet? And he answered, No. Then said they unto 22
him, Who art thou? that we may give an answer to them
that sent us. What sayest thou of thyself? He said, I am 23
the voice of one crying in the wilderness, Make straight
the way of the Lord, as said the prophet Esaias.[2] And 24
they which were sent were of the Pharisees. And they 25
asked him, and said unto him, Why baptizest thou then,
if thou be not that Christ, nor Elias, neither that
prophet? John answered them, saying, I baptize with 26
water:[3] but there standeth one among you, whom ye
know not; he it is, who coming after me is preferred 27
before me, whose shoe's latchet I am not worthy to
unloose. These things were done in Bethabara beyond 28
Jordan, where John was baptizing.

The next day John seeth Jesus coming unto him, 29

[1] Cf. Mk. ix. 13.   [2] Cf. Mk. i. 3.
[3] Cf. Mk. i. 8; Q, p. 163 (Lk. iii. 16).

and saith, Behold the Lamb of God, which taketh away
30 the sin of the world. This is he of whom I said, After
me cometh a man which is preferred before me: for he
31 was before me. And I knew him not: but that he
should be made manifest to Israel, therefore am I come
32 baptizing with water. And John bare record, saying,
I saw the Spirit descending from heaven like a dove,
33 and it abode upon him.[1] And I knew him not: but he
that sent me to baptize with water, the same said unto
me, Upon whom thou shalt see the Spirit descending,
and remaining on him, the same is he which baptizeth
34 with the Holy Ghost. And I saw, and bare record that
this is the Son of God.

II. THE CALL OF THE FIRST DISCIPLES

35 Again the next day after John stood, and two of his
36 disciples; and looking upon Jesus as he walked, he saith,
37 Behold the Lamb of God! And the two disciples heard
38 him speak, and they followed Jesus. Then Jesus turned,
and saw them following, and saith unto them, What seek
ye? They said unto him, Rabbi, (which is to say, being
39 interpreted, Master,) where dwellest thou? He saith
unto them, Come and see. They came and saw where
he dwelt, and abode with him that day: for it was
40 about the tenth hour. One of the two which heard
John speak, and followed him, was Andrew, Simon
41 Peter's brother.[2] He first findeth his own brother
Simon, and saith unto him, We have found the Messias,

[1] Cf. Mk. i. 10.   [2] Cf. Mk. i. 16.

which is, being interpreted, the Christ. And he brought 42
him to Jesus. And when Jesus beheld him, he said,
Thou art Simon the son of Jona: thou shalt be called
Cephas, which is by interpretation, A stone.[1]

III. FIRST WORK IN GALILEE

The day following Jesus would go forth into Galilee, 43
and findeth Philip, and saith unto him, Follow me.
Now Philip was of Bethsaida, the city of Andrew and 44
Peter. Philip findeth Nathanael, and saith unto him, We 45
have found him, of whom Moses in the law, and the
prophets, did write, Jesus of Nazareth, the son of
Joseph. And Nathanael said unto him, Can there any 46
good thing come out of Nazareth? Philip saith unto
him, Come and see. Jesus saw Nathanael coming to 47
him, and saith of him, Behold an Israelite indeed, in
whom is no guile! Nathanael saith unto him, Whence 48
knowest thou me? Jesus answered and said unto him,
Before that Philip called thee, when thou wast under the
fig tree, I saw thee. Nathanael answered and saith unto 49
him, Rabbi, thou art the Son of God; thou art the King
of Israel. Jesus answered and said unto him, Because I 50
said unto thee, I saw thee under the fig tree, believest
thou? thou shalt see greater things than these. And he 51
saith unto him, Verily, verily, I say unto you, Hereafter
ye shall see heaven open, and the angels of God
ascending and descending upon the Son of man.[2]

[1] Cf. Mk. iii. 16.   [2] Cf. pp. 83–4, 95; Mk. iii. 10, etc.

2 1 And the third day there was a marriage in Cana of Galilee;
2 and the mother of Jesus was there: and both Jesus
3 was called, and his disciples, to the marriage. And when
they wanted wine, the mother of Jesus saith unto him,
4 They have no wine. Jesus saith unto her, Woman,
what have I to do with thee?[1] mine hour is not yet
5 come. His mother saith unto the servants, Whatsoever
6 he saith unto you, do it. And there were set there six
waterpots of stone, after the manner of the purifying of
7 the Jews, containing two or three firkins apiece. Jesus
saith unto them, Fill the waterpots with water. And
8 they filled them up to the brim. And he saith unto them,
Draw out now, and bear unto the governor of the feast.
9 And they bare it. When the ruler of the feast had tasted
the water that was made wine, and knew not whence
it was: (but the servants which drew the water knew;)
10 the governor of the feast called the bridegroom, and
saith unto him, Every man at the beginning doth set
forth good wine; and when men have well drunk, then
that which is worse: but thou hast kept the good wine
11 until now. This beginning of miracles did Jesus in
Cana of Galilee, and manifested forth his glory; and his
disciples believed on him.

12   After this he went down to Capernaum, he, and his
mother, and his brethren, and his disciples: and they
continued there not many days.

[1] Cf. Mk. iii. 33.

IV. A PASSOVER IN JERUSALEM
(cf. Mk. xi. 15–18)

And the Jews' passover was at hand, and Jesus went 13
up to Jerusalem, and found in the temple those that 14
sold oxen and sheep and doves, and the changers of
money sitting: and when he had made a scourge of 15
small cords, he drove them all out of the temple, and the
sheep, and the oxen; and poured out the changers'
money, and overthrew the tables; and said unto them 16
that sold doves, Take these things hence; make not my
Father's house an house of merchandise. And his dis- 17
ciples remembered that it was written, The zeal of
thine house hath eaten me up.

Then answered the Jews and said unto him, What 18
sign shewest thou unto us, seeing that thou doest these
things? Jesus answered and said unto them, Destroy 19
this temple, and in three days I will raise it up.[1] Then 20
said the Jews, Forty and six years[2] was this temple in
building, and wilt thou rear it up in three days? But he 21
spake of the temple of his body. When therefore he 22
was risen from the dead, his disciples remembered
that he had said this unto them; and they believed the
scripture, and the word which Jesus had said.

Now when he was in Jerusalem at the passover, in 23
the feast day, many believed in his name, when they saw
the miracles which he did. But Jesus did not commit 24
himself unto them, because he knew all men, and 25

[1] Cf. Mk. xiv. 58.
[2] Herod's rebuilding began in 20 B.C.

needed not that any should testify of man: for he knew what was in man.

[Here follows the discourse with Nicodemus.]

V. JOHN AND JESUS

3 22   After these things came Jesus and his disciples into the land of Judæa; and there he tarried with them, and baptized.

23   And John also was baptizing in Ænon near to Salim, because there was much water there: and they came, and 24 were baptized. For John was not yet cast into prison.[1]

25   Then there arose a question between some of John's 26 disciples and the Jews about purifying. And they came unto John, and said unto him, Rabbi, he that was with thee beyond Jordan, to whom thou barest witness, behold, the same baptizeth, and all men come to him. 27 John answered and said, A man can receive nothing, 28 except it be given him from heaven. Ye yourselves bear me witness, that I said, I am not the Christ, but that I am 29 sent before him. He that hath the bride is the bridegroom:[2] but the friend of the bridegroom, which standeth and heareth him, rejoiceth greatly because of the bridegroom's voice: this my joy therefore is fulfilled. 30 He must increase, but I must decrease.

[1] Cf. pp. 53–4.
[2] Cf. Mk. ii. 19.

VI. IN SAMARIA

4 When therefore the Lord knew how the Pharisees had ₁
heard that Jesus made and baptized more disciples than
John, (though Jesus himself baptized not, but his dis- ₂
ciples,) he left Judæa, and departed again into Galilee. ₃
And he must needs go through Samaria. Then cometh ₄, ₅
he to a city of Samaria, which is called Sychar, near to
the parcel of ground that Jacob gave to his son Joseph.
Now Jacob's well was there. Jesus therefore, being ₆
wearied with his journey, sat thus on the well: and it was
about the sixth hour. There cometh a woman of Samaria ₇
to draw water: Jesus saith unto her, Give me to drink.

Here follows the discourse to the Woman of Samaria.

And many of the Samaritans of that city believed on ₃₉
him for the saying of the woman, which testified, He
told me all that ever I did. So when the Samaritans ₄₀
were come unto him, they besought him that he would
tarry with them: and he abode there two days. And ₄₁
many more believed because of his own word; and said ₄₂
unto the woman, Now we believe, not because of thy
saying: for we have heard him ourselves, and know that
this is indeed the Christ, the Saviour of the world.

VII. IN GALILEE
(cf. Q, pp. 168-9)

43 Now after two days Jesus departed thence, and went
44 into Galilee. For he himself testified, that a prophet
45 hath no honour in his own country.[1] Then when he
was come into Galilee, the Galilæans received him,
having seen all the things that he did at Jerusalem at
46 the feast: for they also went unto the feast. So Jesus
came again into Cana of Galilee, where he made the
water wine. And there was a certain nobleman,[2] whose
47 son was sick at Capernaum. When he heard that Jesus
was come out of Judæa into Galilee, he went unto him,
and besought him that he would come down, and heal
48 his son: for he was at the point of death. Then said
Jesus unto him, Except ye see signs and wonders, ye
49 will not believe. The nobleman saith unto him, Sir,
50 come down ere my child die. Jesus saith unto him, Go
thy way; thy son liveth. And the man believed the word
that Jesus had spoken unto him, and he went his way.
51 And as he was now going down, his servants met him,
52 and told him, saying, Thy son liveth. Then inquired he
of them the hour when he began to amend. And they
said unto him, Yesterday at the seventh hour the fever
53 left him. So the father knew that it was at the same
hour, in the which Jesus said unto him, Thy son liveth:
54 and himself believed, and his whole house. This is again
the second miracle that Jesus did, when he was come
out of Judæa into Galilee.

[1] Cf. Mk. vi. 4.
[2] I.e. king's officer, possibly the centurion of Q.

VIII. IN JERUSALEM

5 After this there was a feast of the Jews;[1] and Jesus 1
went up to Jerusalem. Now there is at Jerusalem by the 2
sheep market a pool, which is called in the Hebrew
tongue Bethesda, having five porches. In these lay a 3
great multitude of impotent folk, of blind, halt, withered,
waiting for the moving of the water. For an angel went 4
down at a certain season into the pool, and troubled the
water: whosoever then first after the troubling of the
water stepped in was made whole of whatsoever disease
he had. And a certain man was there, which had an 5
infirmity thirty and eight years. When Jesus saw him 6
lie, and knew that he had been now a long time in that
case, he saith unto him, Wilt thou be made whole? The 7
impotent man answered him, Sir, I have no man, when
the water is troubled, to put me into the pool: but while
I am coming, another steppeth down before me. Jesus 8
saith unto him, Rise, take up thy bed, and walk. And 9
immediately the man was made whole, and took up his
bed, and walked: and on the same day was the sabbath.

The Jews therefore said unto him that was cured, It 10
is the sabbath day: it is not lawful for thee to carry thy
bed. He answered them, He that made me whole, the 11
same said unto me, Take up thy bed, and walk. Then 12
asked they him, What man is that which said unto thee,
Take up thy bed, and walk? And he that was healed 13
wist not who it was: for Jesus had conveyed himself
away, a multitude being in that place. Afterward Jesus 14

[1] Possibly this and the following chapter have been transposed.
If so, this feast will be the Passover of vi. 4.

findeth him in the temple, and said unto him, Behold,
thou art made whole: sin no more, lest a worse thing
15 come unto thee. The man departed, and told the Jews
16 that it was Jesus, which had made him whole. And
therefore did the Jews persecute Jesus, and sought to slay
him, because he had done these things on the sabbath
day.[1]

IX. IN GALILEE

6 1 After these things Jesus went over the sea of Galilee,
2 which is the sea of Tiberias. And a great multitude
followed him, because they saw his miracles which he
3 did on them that were diseased. And Jesus went up
into a mountain, and there he sat with his disciples.
4 And the passover, a feast of the Jews, was nigh.

5   When Jesus then lifted up his eyes, and saw a great
company come unto him, he saith unto Philip, Whence
6 shall we buy bread, that these may eat?[2] And this he
said to prove him: for he himself knew what he would
7 do. Philip answered him, Two hundred pennyworth
of bread is not sufficient for them, that every one of
8 them may take a little. One of his disciples, Andrew,
9 Simon Peter's brother, saith unto him, There is a lad
here, which hath five barley loaves, and two small fishes:
10 but what are they among so many? And Jesus said,
Make the men sit down. Now there was much grass in
the place. So the men sat down, in number about five
11 thousand. And Jesus took the loaves; and when he had
given thanks, he distributed to the disciples, and the

[1] This section has points of contact with Mk. ii. 1–12 and iii. 1–6.
[2] Cf. Mk. vi. 30–44.

disciples to them that were set down; and likewise of the
fishes as much as they would. When they were filled, 12
he said unto his disciples, Gather up the fragments that
remain, that nothing be lost. Therefore they gathered 13
them together, and filled twelve baskets with the
fragments of the five barley loaves, which remained
over and above unto them that had eaten. Then those 14
men, when they had seen the miracle that Jesus did,
said, This is of a truth that prophet that should come
into the world.

When Jesus therefore perceived that they would come 15
and take him by force, to make him a king, he departed
again into a mountain himself alone. And when even 16
was now come, his disciples went down unto the sea,[1]
and entered into a ship, and went over the sea toward 17
Capernaum. And it was now dark, and Jesus was not
come to them. And the sea arose by reason of a great 18
wind that blew. So when they had rowed about five 19
and twenty or thirty furlongs, they see Jesus walking on
the sea, and drawing nigh unto the ship: and they were
afraid. But he saith unto them, It is I; be not afraid. 20
Then they willingly received[2] him into the ship: and 21
immediately the ship was at the land whither they went.

The day following, when the people which stood on 22
the other side of the sea saw that there was none other
boat there, save that one whereinto his disciples were
entered, and that Jesus went not with his disciples into
the boat, but that his disciples were gone away alone;
(howbeit there came other boats from Tiberias nigh 23

---

[1] Cf. Mk. vi. 45–52.
[2] Lit. "were wishing to receive."

unto the place where they did eat bread, after that the
24 Lord had given thanks:) when the people therefore saw
that Jesus was not there, neither his disciples, they also
took shipping, and came to Capernaum, seeking for
25 Jesus. And when they had found him on the other side
of the sea, they said unto him, Rabbi, when camest thou
26 hither? Jesus answered them and said, Verily, verily,
I say unto you, Ye seek me, not because ye saw the
miracles, but because ye did eat of the loaves, and were
27 filled. Labour not for the meat which perisheth, but for
that meat which endureth unto everlasting life, which the
Son of man shall give unto you: for him hath God the
28 Father sealed. Then said they unto him, What shall
29 we do, that we might work the works of God? Jesus
answered and said unto them, This is the work of God,
that ye believe on him whom he hath sent.

Here follows the discourse on the Bread of Life.

66   From that time many of his disciples went back,
67 and walked no more with him. Then said Jesus unto
68 the twelve, Will ye also go away? Then Simon Peter
answered him, Lord, to whom shall we go? thou hast the
69 words of eternal life. And we believe and are sure that
70 thou art that Christ, the Son of the living God.[1] Jesus
answered them, Have not I chosen you twelve, and one
71 of you is a devil? He spake of Judas Iscariot the son of
Simon: for he it was that should betray him, being one
of the twelve.
7 1 After these things Jesus walked in Galilee: for he would
not walk in Jewry, because the Jews sought to kill him.

[1] Cf. Mk. viii. 29.

Now the Jews' feast of tabernacles was at hand. His 2, 3
brethren therefore said unto him, Depart hence, and
go into Judæa, that thy disciples also may see the
works that thou doest. For there is no man that doeth 4
any thing in secret, and he himself seeketh to be known
openly. If thou do these things, shew thyself to the
world. For neither did his brethren believe in him. 5
Then Jesus said unto them, My time is not yet come: 6
but your time is alway ready. The world cannot hate 7
you; but me it hateth, because I testify of it, that the
works thereof are evil. Go ye up unto this feast: I go 8
not up yet unto this feast; for my time is not yet full
come. When he had said these words unto them, he 9
abode still in Galilee.

But when his brethren were gone up, then went 10
he also up unto the feast, not openly, but as it were
in secret.

[The rest of the Gospel is concerned with events and
teaching in Judæa and Jerusalem: for its sequence cf. p. 69.
It bears no resemblance to the Synoptists until ch. xii, the
Anointing at Bethany (cf. Mk. xiv. 3–9) and the Triumphal
Entry (Mk. xi. 1–10).]

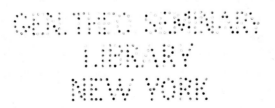

CAMBRIDGE: PRINTED BY
WALTER LEWIS, M.A.
AT THE UNIVERSITY PRESS